The Seven Stories
of Love

Marcia Millman

♥

The Seven Stories of Love

AND HOW TO CHOOSE YOUR HAPPY ENDING

wm WILLIAM MORROW 75 Years of Publishing
An Imprint of HarperCollinsPublishers

FIRST EDITION

Designed by Gretchen Achilles

Printed on acid-free paper

Library of Congress Cataloging-in-Publication Data has been applied for.

ISBN 0-688-17200-8

01   02   03   04   05   QW   10   9   8   7   6   5   4   3   2   1

FOR WAYNE A. MYERS

*Character gives us qualities, but it is in our actions—what we do—that
we are happy or the reverse.*

—ARISTOTLE, *The Poetics*

[Life] is all one great big movie. But you can't pick your genre.

—SKEET ULRICH as BILLY LOOMIS in *Scream*

Contents

The Seven Stories
of Love

Introduction

We live out our lives as stories—especially those parts of our lives that involve love.

After two decades of teaching, researching, and interviewing, and observing hundreds of people on this subject, I have come to recognize that most of us enact our romantic relationships through seven basic stories. I've also discovered that each of us has a primary love story that we repeat throughout our lives, either with one partner or in different relationships. In addition, our primary story determines our choice of partners and how we behave at critical turning points. Sometimes we notice repetitive patterns in our love relationships, but few of us ever recognize our grand scenario, even though it dominates our lives. Our stories are determined by early experiences, but fortunately we can choose to rewrite their ending once we recognize and understand them.

Poor communication or low self-esteem is usually said to be the cause of problems in a romantic relationship. I have found neither of these concepts to be helpful. The biggest problem in most love affairs is that people don't realize they repeatedly enact the same unconscious love story, which also directs their behavior and choice of partners. This is why our romantic relationships often seem to operate beyond our control or move in directions that make us unhappy.

This book should help you recognize and understand your unconscious scenarios, as well as their source and their hidden meanings. I'll show you that behind each of the major seven love stories is some event or circumstance early in your life—in your childhood or adolescence—that fuels your attraction to particular romantic plots. Once you recognize your story and understand where it comes from, you can exercise greater control. Instead of feeling trapped in the same nightmare over and over, you'll be able to choose your happiest ending.

As I will show you, a love story is more than finding the right partner and living with him or her happily ever after. It also involves your desire to master the major losses or traumas you encountered in life, especially in your childhood, and in relation to your parents. Love can either help you to grow and resolve your problems, or it can cruelly repeat the original disappointment, confirming your worst fears.

Romantic love is not a sickness or an illusion, as some people like to argue. Even repeating a particular scenario is not a sign of pathology. Like the heroine of *Run Lola Run,* some of us need to repeat our story a few times, before it comes out right.

Self-esteem does play a large role in our experience of love, but it takes very different forms in different scenarios. It's not useful to say that love problems are caused by low self-esteem because many strong and self-confident people are extremely vulnerable in love. The problems people have with self-esteem in love relationships are very specific to each romantic scenario because they are linked to particular formative experiences in our youth.

Whether we are basically healthy or highly neurotic, most of us are drawn to one particular love story. We are drawn to scenarios that give us the chance to turn back the clock and do something over again in the hope that it will turn out the way we always wanted it to be. And it's not uncommon to repeat a love story over and over because we haven't yet learned how to make it turn out better. This is why at the beginning romantic love often feels like going home and recovering something that was lost. But we want to return to an idealized home, where the painful aspects of our childhood have been resolved or removed.

We never completely exhaust the quest to recover our idealized past because we want to feel connected to our childhood, with its open possibilities. In particular, we want to undo something that went wrong, to feel in control where we once felt powerless. Romantic love is a powerful way of going back, and we are drawn to particular love stories because they call us back to something unresolved or problematic that we need to repeat.

Each of the seven stories of love revolves around a specific problem or trauma, and different versions of each story can teach us why some people grow and find happiness in love, while others become more anxious or depressed.

As I will show you, there's usually more than one plot being played out between two people. We don't find someone who can simply play the costarring role in our favorite romantic scenario. Usually our partner is playing out his own story, and he may have cast us in a role we might not appreciate. People always get into trouble when they don't look objectively at their partners and ask what story their partner is living in. They put themselves at risk when they ignore the warning signs and the aspects of their lover's behavior that make them uneasy. In addition to learning about our own romantic scenarios we need to examine our partner's repetitive dramas, and ask whether this is a story we can live with.

Is Love a Cure-all?

Love can be a healing experience because it gives people a chance to overcome specific traumas from childhood. It's also a general cure-all for many existential problems, like anxiety over death or being alone. It has this beneficial effect because love restores the feelings of connection and being watched over—it brings back the sense of safety we might have once felt as a child. It makes us feel we have recovered something crucial that we lost from the past. These healing properties of love enhance our self-esteem because we feel connected to something powerful and benevolent.

If love can do all this, why do some people seem compelled to repeat a painful or disappointing scenario over and over? It is often assumed, incorrectly, they are masochists who want to punish themselves. But this is rarely the case. Very few people repeat unhappy love stories because they want to suffer. Instead they are trying to master some painful experience from the past. They keep returning to situations that resemble the original trauma in an attempt to make it come out better. They also return to these painful attachments because they are wired into them, and their behavior is just automatic.

We've all seen images of ducklings that become "imprinted" and permanently attached to the human beings who first took care of them. Forever after, those ducklings follow the human figures that are permanently etched in their memories, even though they are not right for them. In the same way, some lovers are imprinted with an early trauma and chase that image forever—even though that choice will never make them happy. They follow that image as unthinkingly as the ducklings.

Your primary love story reveals the issues from your past that you need to resolve in order to find happiness in love. When you understand your story you can make better choices.

How I Discovered the Seven Stories of Love

Over a long period of teaching and researching the subject, I came to recognize and understand the seven major stories. About twenty years ago, I began teaching a college course on the sociology of romantic love. During two decades I have learned a great deal from reading and discussing thousands of students' papers. Teaching these classes has given me a chance to see how different generations of young adults experience and think about love.

To prepare for my courses and lectures, I've also spent years reflecting on classic and contemporary romantic movies and books. It is often said that Hollywood gives people unrealistic images of romantic love, but I believe our favorite romantic movies actually reveal our wishes and fears even more than they shape them.

One of the pleasures of watching movies is being able to live through the characters and thereby have an emotional catharsis. Movies evoke powerful feelings and let us open up to undying hopes or sadnesses about losses we have never recovered from. The happy endings of movies like *An Affair to Remember* or *Pretty Woman* may not be realistic, but they still reflect our deepest wishes.

I found that examining the plots of movies was the way to get my students to think about romantic patterns and scenarios. My students could see the repeated themes so clearly, and in the darkness of the theater, their publicly cynical postures could not stand up to their strong emotional identification with the characters and the stories.

Some of my students proclaim their skepticism about romantic love in class discussions. In other courses they've been taught that romantic love is a product of capitalist consumption, or an ideology that reinforces the subjugation of women. Half of them had watched their parents divorce. But in their papers, almost all of them admit to having the fantasies they publicly ridicule. In a recent batch of papers I received on romantic fantasies or experiences, only one student in over a hundred said she hoped she would never fall in love. As we'll see, even cynics are living out a romantic scenario they don't understand.

Recently, a number of my students have begun saying that their ideal partner would be a former friend, one they had first known platonically for many many years. I wondered what this could possibly mean. Was this a new love scenario that I needed to investigate? Or do young people feel they can't trust their judgments about romantic partners? Do they really think they need five years of dispassionate observing, uncontaminated by sex, to make a sensible choice?

Upon further inquiry, I learned that my students who wanted to marry or become the lover of their long-term best friend have never achieved this. Actually, they were just rationalizing a common romantic problem: *avoidance* of real romantic involvement through unrequited longings for someone who isn't interested or available.

But I do think my students were expressing something important: many of us find it difficult to look at our romantic partners or situations objectively, so we make serious mistakes. I couldn't agree with them more. But the answer to that problem is not to avoid romantic love, but to learn how to take a fully honest look at our partners and our own behavior. We need to evaluate romantic partners and situations objectively. We need to ask questions and gather as much information as possible in order to choose the partner who will make us happy.

For the most part, the papers my students write describe the same fantasies and scenarios that Hollywood keeps updating, and these stories are often contemporary versions of ones written by Jane Austen, Charlotte Brontë, Henry James, Tolstoy, or Pushkin. These same stories are retold by contemporary fiction writers. The seemingly infinite varieties of love may fall within a limited number of plots. As I kept seeing the same themes turn up in all these different places—Hollywood movies, contemporary and nineteenth-century fiction, my undergraduate students' papers—I started to realize that there are only so many love stories. And they are always unconscious reenactments or responses to traumas that are common in childhood and adolescence: for example, a parent's early sickness or death, a father's coldness and disapproval, or a mother who made her child take care of her.

Though Jane Austen never married and Charlotte Brontë married only shortly before she died both wrote love stories that have been imitated and rewritten for almost two centuries. In romantic love, there isn't much difference between the stories that are lived and those created in the imagination, because both are built around the same unconscious needs and fantasies.

During two decades of research on gender and women's experiences, I have talked with over a hundred women about their experiences with love. To confirm my ideas about the psychological origins of different romantic scenarios and to learn more about them, I've interviewed therapists and psychoanalysts, who probably have the best view into this process. While writing this book I continued to interview more women and to test my observations about the childhood origins of each of the seven stories. The links between particular love scenarios and formative life experiences are remarkably consistent.

I have drawn from all these sources—interviews (with names and identities changed), movies, and novels—to present the seven stories to you. I have written only of heterosexual romance, with some regret, because I suspect the scenarios played out by gay and lesbian lovers are substantially similar. Ultimately, I decided that analysis needs the insight of writers who can also draw from their own experiences.

This book will help you understand the characteristic conflicts and challenges of each romantic scenario. And it will help you recognize and understand the ones that prevail in your life. Unfortunately, our stories are rarely easy for us to see because they always contain elements of self-deception or denial.

Even more important, this book will help you see the choices you've made without being aware of them. We can't pick our love stories, any more than we can change our childhood. But once we learn our basic story we can learn how to choose the right partner. We can also learn to recognize the story our partner is playing out and decide if we want to live with that scenario. We can learn to exercise choice and control over these stories so that we can direct them, instead of helplessly following their course.

Before looking at each story in depth, I want to give you a brief description of all seven major romantic plots. I've put them roughly in the chronological order of when they become prominent in life. Our primary love stories usually stay with us forever, because they are responses to early experiences that had a deep impact on our development. Many of us also live through secondary love plots: the ones our partners are caught up in, or stories that emerge as we pass through different stages of life.

The Seven Stories in Brief

1. FIRST LOVE

The story of first love is about trying to separate from our parents—becoming independent from them and allowing ourselves to become different from them. Usually we choose our first love on the basis of what we need in order to accomplish this separation. It's the underlying theme of movies like *Dirty Dancing* and *Titanic*.

Some of us pick a partner who is very different from our parents or someone our parents would strongly disapprove of. If we don't feel guilty about leaving our parents we may pick someone different and allow ourselves pleasure in the relationship. A person who feels guilty about leaving her parents may choose someone different, but she's not as likely to end up happy.

Others choose a first lover who comes from a similar background, or at least, a partner their parents regard as ideal. This allows them to avoid feeling separated from their parents. Their married life is barely distinguishable from what they grew up with.

Guilt about separating from parents is very common, whether it's conscious or not. It is generated by parents who don't give us permission to leave—who let us know that if we left them to pursue our own happiness, they would be seriously harmed. Children raised with this message often rebel by choosing a partner from a different world. This person helps them make a difficult break. But sometimes guilt leads them to choose a partner who doesn't treat them well—

this is their self-punishment for defying their parents. As I'll show, when parents don't give their child permission to become independent, their child must get that permission from another source before they can find happiness in love.

But in any case, our first love is really a transitional object, someone who fits with our particular needs and approach to dealing with the separation from parents. We choose our first love out of this need, even in cases where a first love turns into a lasting relationship.

Later in life, the story of First Love often becomes important again. In middle and late age, when we regret the loss of youth, it's common to fantasize about reuniting with someone you knew or loved when you were young. Even though they have also grown older, they remember us in our youth and shared it to some degree. We see our young selves reflected in their eyes—and they allow us to connect to the person we once were, when we felt that anything and everything was possible.

Like all the other romantic scenarios, the later-life fantasy about reunion with a first love represents a wish to turn back the clock, recapture our own youth, and make things turn out differently. We want to reconnect to a time when our love felt pure and unspoiled by calculation or cynicism. Or we want to go back to win the person we could only love from a distance in our youth, because at that time they wouldn't have looked at us twice or we didn't have the self-confidence to try.

2. PYGMALION

This story, very common among younger women, involves finding a parental substitute who can give her the practical knowledge for succeeding in the world—knowledge her parents did not or could not provide. She chooses a lover who is also a teacher or mentor—someone she admires who could help her develop her own talents or potential.

The mentor relationship and the Pygmalion love story have

much in common, and what starts as a mentor-protégée relationship may turn into a romantic connection. The older lover and the younger have different needs, but if they are complementary, this union can be happy and lasting. For this love relationship to work, the mentor must see the protégée as more than the reflected glory of his own brilliance—more than the magnificent statue he created from a lump a clay. He must also understand that he can't control her, and that in teaching her, he has helped her not only to become an equal but also to be less dependent on him. The protégée must love her mentor for reasons other than what he can teach her, or else she will always be discarding her mentors after she's outgrown them, or extracted what she needs from them, moving on to new mentors who are bigger and better.

3. OBSESSIVE LOVE

This is about trying to rid yourself of the rage you experienced (and could not express) if you felt either abandoned by your parents or excessively controlled by them. Perhaps a parent died or left you. Or your parents were so controlling they made you feel passive and at their mercy. Obsessive lovers repeat the story of control or abandonment in their adult relationships. If they were controlled, they may want to control back. If they were abandoned, they feel annihilated when a lover leaves. They'll do anything to keep the relationship alive, even if it exists only in their own imaginations.

Obsessive relationships lead to a wide range of reactions—from self-abasement, to stalking and threats, to falling into a deep depression. Most of all, obsessive lovers want to cleanse themselves of the rage that they felt toward their parents. Unconsciously, they feel that securing the love of a person they've idealized will erase that anger and make everything okay. But they rarely pick a partner who will cooperate with their plan.

Many people experience romantic obsessions at some point in life, but this occurs most often in youth, when a sense of identity and boundaries are not highly developed. The loss of a lover with whom you have merged your identity makes you feel totally annihilated. This feels unbearable, which is why an obsessive lover hangs on to a beloved as if he or she were hanging on to life. Some young people outgrow this pattern when their identity solidifies—a romantic rejection is then less devastating. Other people repeat the story to greater and greater extremes. They are the full-fledged obsessive lovers. The extreme scenario of obsessive love has been depicted in movies like *Fatal Attraction*. But the real meaning of the story is almost always misunderstood. The obsessive lover's problem isn't loving too much (as it's sometimes portrayed) but rather hating too much, and trying to disguise and escape from her rage.

Of all the seven stories, this one is the hardest to bring to a happy conclusion unless the lover changes herself—by finding a way to gain self-esteem that doesn't depend on merging with a lover, and then needing to control him.

4. THE DOWNSTAIRS WOMAN AND THE UPSTAIRS MAN

This love plot is a kind of Cinderella story that has a wide romantic appeal and is retold in classic novels like Jane Austen's *Pride and Prejudice,* Charlotte Brontë's *Jane Eyre,* and Daphne du Maurier's *Rebecca,* as well as in popular movies like *Pretty Woman.*

A woman falls in love with a man who at first doesn't take her seriously because she doesn't belong to his social world. The man must come to see her natural superiority despite her humble background. And she must learn to overcome her anger at his greater power—an intimidating power that also attracts her. The psychological origin of this story is usually not appreciated: this romantic scenario is usually motivated by a relationship with a cold or rejecting father who made us feel unworthy. In adulthood, the daughter tries to win the love of a powerful man who initially treats her dismissively. She struggles to maintain her pride and to make him aware of her superior qualities. She also tries to uncover the tenderness that lies beneath his cold exterior. Her talents and independence have usually separated her from her past, and she feels unconnected and alone. She wants her lover to give her a place in the world where she can feel she belongs.

5. SACRIFICE

This story (the theme of *Casablanca, The End of the Affair, The Bridges of Madison County, The Horse Whisperer*) is about the conflict between duty and passion, the choice between personal happiness and serving the needs of others. A middle-aged woman who is already married, often with children, a woman who has always led a measured and controlled existence, unexpectedly meets her soul mate and falls passionately in love. She is torn between love and not wanting to hurt others, especially her children. Afraid that her love would never survive her guilt, and fearing the damage it would cause, she sacrifices her love and her personal happiness to avoid hurting others. That is the obvious story.

Beneath the nobility of her renunciation of happiness there is also her fear and guilt. She is terrified that her intense feelings will make her feel out of control. She is afraid to give up the safe, controlled life she has led as well as the social context and conventions that support her. Risking everything for one intense love frightens her.

6. RESCUE

In this very common love story, a woman chooses a lover who has been wounded and must be nursed back to health. The heroine will prove she can restore him to his original or potential greatness with her infinite patience and love. She sees in him what no one else sees—the prince hidden within the tattered man. The story of rescue has been wrongly reduced to images of women who are "codependent" or women who love men who are unworthy: incorrigible alcoholics or abusive, exploitative men.

In fact, rescue is an element in many mutually rewarding relationships. But the psychological origin of this story is almost never recognized: in childhood, a girl lost a father she loved—through death, illness, or divorce. Unconsciously, she blames her mother for the loss of her father. The rescue and recovery of her lover is also an effort to resurrect the father she lost, and to show she is more loving and competent than her mother.

Unconsciously, she hopes her restored lover will give her the protection she missed from her father. So rescuing her lover is actually motivated by the wish to be rescued herself. In classic tales of rescue, like *Beauty and the Beast*, contemporary movies like *Run Lola Run*, and novels like *The Girl's Guide to Hunting and Fishing,* the heroine is always racing between her wounded lover and her dying father because unconsciously they are closely connected. This love story can be very gratifying if the woman picks a partner who deserves her efforts and if she doesn't require him to become her savior.

Rescue is also a very common love story for men. For some, it can end in a mutually satisfying relationship that makes them feel like heros. Other men who are drawn to the rescue scenario suffer from dividing women into madonnas and whores. They feel sexually aroused or at ease only with a woman who is fallen, depressed, or in serious trouble—but they feel these women are unsuitable for marriage.

For many people, the rescue plot is the primary love scenario. But the feeling of rescue is present in most romantic relationships, and certainly most happy ones, because people who find happiness in love usually feel they've been saved or that they've recovered something wonderful they had lost.

7. THE COURAGE TO LOVE: OVERCOMING POSTPONEMENT AND AVOIDANCE

This is about realizing that you don't have forever to get what you want. This story, illustrated by the movies *An Affair to Remember, Sleepless in Seattle,* and *Forever Young,* is about the willingness to take a big risk for love, and having the faith that things will work out. The hero or heroine must struggle against their tendency to avoid intimacy and commitment. The story is tied to the recognition of mortality. People who avoid getting romantically involved often live in a fantasy that they will stay forever young. They won't acknowledge that time is passing, and unconsciously they think that avoiding commitment will keep them from growing old. Others cynically avoid love by believing that everyone else is hopelessly flawed and naive. Avoiders, postponers, and cynics share many qualities—most notably, they are living as if time is suspended.

People who live out this scenario fall in love only after they are forced to fully confront the reality of time and mortality. The feeling that it's now or never—that this is really their last or only chance—shakes them loose from their indecision. When they get over their inhibition, they become so aware of time running out that they typically race to beat the clock.

In the end, finding the courage to love is more likely to give us a feeling of immortality because it makes us feel connected, and through that connection we will always live on in the people we have loved. In contrast, people who avoid commitment usually discover they've lost their lives because they have watched the important experiences from the sidelines, so their lives have gone by unlived.

Our love stories are based on deeply formative experiences, so we can't always change them, any more than we can erase our past. Our story is part of who we are. We need to accept it, and we need to learn how to get the greatest happiness out of it.

Romantic attraction is tied to our stories. This is why you might feel totally "bored" by someone who looks great to everyone else, while someone who seems a little crazy to your friends is absolutely fascinating and wonderful to you. The person who doesn't resonate with your love story is boring, and the one who does is exciting. The excitement comes when a person resonates with your drama, providing the chance to revisit a formative trauma and come out victorious. But living within any story also offers many choices—in partners and behavior—and the happiest people are those who have learned to make the best choices.

Sometimes we do outgrow a story when a need is met. For example, once we've separated from parents, we don't need a partner who offers an escape route. Most other love stories, like Rescue, Obsession, Sacrifice, and Upstairs-Downstairs, are rarely outgrown because they are based on experiences that leave a more permanent mark or inclination. But that doesn't mean we can't exercise choice within each scenario. Every story has crucial turning points when we are offered several options—especially which partner to choose from among those who fit into our drama, and how to respond when certain conflicts emerge. The more we understand our story, the more likely we are to bring it to a happy resolution.

For example, both men and women live out the love story of Rescue. Women who lost beloved fathers early in life are often attracted to men who allow them to revisit this trauma. But a Rescue scenario may lead to different choices and outcomes. A woman may choose a man who thrives on her love. He brings other strengths and shared interests to the relationship, so their union is built on more than his wounds and her efforts to make him whole. The Rescue element in their relationship provides emotional intensity and resonance—it's a powerful glue that can actually be gratifying to both. Their love both redeems and strengthens them.

Another woman who is drawn to the Rescue plot may choose a partner who is a dedicated alcoholic who has no intention of changing. Maybe he has other attractive qualities, but eventually they are lost in all the troubles he creates by his drinking. Not only does he exploit her generosity, but eventually he'll accuse her of being castrating, controlling, and nagging. And he'll blame her for his problems. Aside from all the misery he causes, this relationship is not going to make her feel she gained mastery over the sorrow of her youth. This husband won't give her the satisfaction that she succeeded where her mother failed.

The story of Rescue, like all the seven stories, has many possible endings. It can be wonderfully satisfying if you pick a worthy, responsive person, not only because love can bring out the best in us, but because it also helps the woman resolve the problems of her youth—the trauma of losing the father she loved, and having a mother who was not a good model.

So why does one woman who is living the Rescue story choose a partner who is worthy of her effort, while another chooses a total loser? It may be blind luck, because most people don't look at their potential partners all that closely, and we often make bad choices when we are young and naive. The second woman may have been enacting a more extreme scenario of Rescue—one she'd repeated many times—that is usually associated with making a poor choice. The first woman may also have a higher level of self-esteem when it comes to love; she would never choose an alcoholic partner even though her story is Rescue.

Whatever level of self-esteem we started with, romantic love can give it a tremendous boost—which is one of its major attractions. Unfortunately, people who need that lift most—people who feel they are deeply unworthy of love—are often drawn to partners who leave them feeling more worthless and empty. You need a certain degree of self-esteem in the first place to make the most rewarding choices in love.

Within every one of the seven stories there are benevolent choices that meet our needs and others that will leave us feeling more anxious and depressed than we were before. In the chapters that follow, I'll show you how to take an objective look at your story, your choices, your partners, and your own behavior. It will put you in control and is absolutely critical to choosing the happy ending—without taking five years to test your partner.

♥

First Love:
Escape and Recapture

Love is now the stardust
Of yesterday
The music
Of the years
Gone by

—"Star Dust," *by* MITCHELL PARISH *and* HOAGY CARMICHAEL

PART ONE: ESCAPE

The story of First Love revolves around two basic themes: separating from our parents and establishing our own identity. These challenges are never totally resolved, and they affect all our love choices, but our first experience of romantic love is especially tied to our need to separate from our parents.

For example, you may choose a lover from a different world, or one your parents don't approve of, as a way of helping you move away from your parents' world and their assumptions. Just asserting your sexuality and becoming intimate with someone from outside the family already moves you some distance away from the confines of your home.

Some people deal with their fears of separating by finding a parental substitute: perhaps an older or idealized figure. And others make a choice that avoids or minimizes the break: they find a partner who keeps them tied into their childhood worlds—a person chosen by their parents or one who grew up in similar circumstances.

Separating from our parents and finding our own identity are closely intertwined because the only way to form our own identities is to question our parents' values. Growth comes from reexamining the beliefs and behaviors we grew up with. You are not exactly like your parents, and adolescence is usually the time when young people need to recognize that difference and become the person they want to be. If you don't examine the values you grew up with, you lose the opportunity to grow beyond what you were given by your parents.

If you choose a partner whose childhood was just like yours—someone your parents might have chosen for you—you are entering into something like an old-fashioned arranged marriage. It's possible that your parents might have chosen someone good for you—most parents would try. And it's not necessary for you to pick someone your parents don't like in order to separate from them. But if you never question their values and assumptions, and you let them decide (directly or indirectly) who your partner will be, you are passing up the opportunity to grow and develop your own identity.

In our culture, which stresses individual freedom, an adolescent is expected to "find" his or her own identity as part of maturing. But some adolescents find this frightening, and many others are inhibited or made to feel guilty by parents who never gave them permission to grow away.

Permission to Separate

By *permission* I mean that parents must allow their children to become independent and different, and eventually to have a life that does not have their parents at the center of it. It's painful for most parents to see their babies finally fly away from the nest. But good parents prepare for this all along—always letting their children separate from them when they are ready and able, always letting their children become their own persons. It happens right from the start, when the little toddler is taking her first steps—which will eventually lead her away.

It's a delicate process, not only because it's painful for the parents, but also because the child has mixed feelings about separating as well. But parents who don't allow their children to separate are giving them the following message: "Your independence from me and your happiness being away from me, or with somebody else, hurts me and does me harm." This is not the kind of message that encourages a child to be happy.

If your parents didn't give you permission to separate, you must find someone else—a peer or a parental surrogate—who will help you feel that leaving them is allowed.

The Continuous Self

All of this enters into the equation when we pick our first loves or subsequent loves. And there's an additional element. One of the reasons we need love is that we need someone to share our lives. We all need someone not only to feel less alone but also because we need a sense of continuity—the feeling that someone has been with us all of our lives and has shared our experiences. People who haven't shared their lives with someone often feel a loss of themselves, because there's no one who reflects their own existence.

In childhood, we experience that continuity by sharing our lives with our parents; in adulthood, it is usually a partner who fills those needs, although it may also be friends or relatives. This is why people who don't have partners often have a harder time recovering from the death of their parents. When their parents die, they have lost the people who remembered them all their lives.

Finally, a first lover and later loves help us to solidify our identities after childhood because it is now they who reflect our existence— apart from our parents—they are the ones who confirm what we have experienced. When adolescents have a hard time breaking away from overpowering parents, they often fall in love with someone "unsuitable" from their parents' point of view, because they need support to move offshore. Others pick someone older and more experienced, in order to feel safe making the break away from home. What they are really doing is picking a parental substitute—which may not be obvious to them because their lover doesn't look or act at all like their parents.

Making the Break

Breaking away from parents is played out in movies like *Titanic* and *Dirty Dancing*, and in part this is why adolescent girls watch these movies over and over. The girl is drawn to the story of a boy from the other side of the tracks who will rescue her from the control of powerful parents: a boy who will love and protect her as much as a parent would—even sacrificing his own life so she might live. Not only does the male figure nobly protect the female, but he also helps her become a woman. Then, having served his purpose, he conveniently disappears, either by graciously bowing out or by dying in order to save her. In any case, he puts her life first, as a parent might do.

The movie *Dirty Dancing*, filmed in 1987 but set back in the 1960s, tells the story of Baby, a brainy, middle-class teenager (played by Jennifer Grey) who spends the summer at a Catskills resort.

Instead of dating the college-bound boys who would please her father (a physician) she sets her sights on a slightly older, lower-class, and sexy dance instructor (Patrick Swayze) for her first love affair. The hero not only teaches her how to dance, but also leads her through the transformation from a clumsy adolescent to an attractive and self-assured young woman.

Like the hero of *Titanic*, the dance teacher is a noble first lover: he liberates Baby from her parents who unfairly malign him, and he also puts himself at risk to protect her. That's why, despite his appearance, he's really a benevolent parental figure. He doesn't look like a parent (which is why the heroine can lust after him), but he's older and wiser, and he's the teacher. Unlike her father, he doesn't make Baby feel guilty about separating from him and moving on after she has learned what she can from him. He's a perfect transitional figure because he allows Baby to grow away from her parents (and ultimately from him) and protects her even while he's her partner in her transformation to a sexual woman.

At the end of the summer, they must part, as the dance instructor realized from the start. She's on her way to a fancy college, and the best he can hope for is a good winter job as a house painter. The movie was written and produced by women, and it reverses the roles in one familiar story of male sexual initiaion—the story of the noble but socially inappropriate woman who is left behind, after she helps the hero become a man. *Dirty Dancing* was a surprise box office success because adolescent girls kept returning to it over and over, as they did to *Titanic*.

Why the First May Not Be the Last

Some people marry their first loves and live happily ever after. It can be wonderful to spend your whole life with someone you grew up with. But first loves don't always last or give us what we had hoped for. For one thing, it's not so easy to escape from parents: we tend to internalize their judgments, and their warnings and commentary often ring in our ears long after they have died. Using a first love to break free of control doesn't always end up the way we expected. Some partners turn out to be even more controlling than our parents were. Sometimes young couples are mismatched in their readiness for commitment: one person wants to secure the attachment and move directly from his parents' home into a marriage—while the other wants to move away from her parents but have a chance to experiment before settling down. Many first marriages break up because they sprang from the need to separate from parents. Eventually, one of the pair realizes his or her spouse is not the one he or she chooses to be with for the rest of his or her life.

The One and Only

One couple I know met and paired off during the first week of their freshman year in college. By forming an attachment within days of leaving home, they avoided the anxiety that most of their classmates had to face, but they also missed the chance to discover their identities on their own. All through college, they spent almost every day together. As graduation approached, Tim wanted Jeannie to marry him, but Jeannie wanted the chance to date other men. Otherwise she felt she'd always wonder if they chose each other because they were afraid to be alone. Tim was hurt and disappointed, but he forgave her.

For the next few years, they stayed in touch, but they dated other people. Eventually, Jeannie realized that Tim was her choice, and they got back together and married. Thirty years later, they've had the great pleasure to be married to someone who shared their youth, but also the chance to have tried other partners. It was fortunate that Tim could accept Jeannie's need to date other men before making a commitment. He didn't need to be the one and only man she had ever known.

This isn't always the case. Many men who have loved only one woman are destructively jealous of the men who preceded them, even when their predecessors have long been out of the picture. They can't stand the thought of sharing their woman with any other man—even a man who is gone. They need to possess her exclusively.

The popular movie *Chasing Amy* tells such a story. The hero, played by Ben Affleck, falls in love with a woman (played by Joey Lauren Adams) who was a lesbian before meeting him, and she falls in love with him. Her lesbian past doesn't bother him at all—in fact, he likes it because, in his mind, her female lovers don't count. It allows him to think of her as a virgin. All goes well until he learns that she also had sex with two boys, simultaneously, years before, when she was in high school. He can't get this image of the sexual trio out of his mind. Now she appears to him as a whore. Finally he hatches a plot to even the score. The heroine is devastated that he can't accept her past, which she is comfortable with, and she also sees he will never get over it. Wisely, she leaves him, though it breaks her heart. And the hero is left with lasting regrets about losing the woman he truly loved.

Destroyed by First Love: The Source

Some people never get over the loss or rejection of their first love—although usually it's because the rejection repeats a childhood trauma involving loss or abandonment. The hero of Emily Brontë's novel, *Wuthering Heights*, is a classic example: Heathcliff is a poor orphan who is rebuffed by his childhood love once she becomes a teenager, and he spends the rest of his life getting revenge. But the wound of her rejection would not have gone so deep if not for his earlier losses. People like Heathcliff often move into Obsessive love scenarios because of their anger. On the surface it appears they were destroyed by their first romantic disappointment, but the fateful blow was actually inflicted long before.

Vulnerable people are destroyed by romantic disappointment

because love is more than a way of freeing ourselves from parents. We also use love to be healed or to have a loss restored—to be recognized or cared for in a way that our parents failed. We idealize our lovers because when we join ourselves with someone we admire it boosts our own self-esteem and identity. When your first love ends in a rejection that powerfully resonates with a childhood trauma, it confirms the original, formative message: you are unworthy of love. After that, some people will not try again.

One classic story along these lines is Henry James's novel *Washington Square* and several movie versions of it (including *The Heiress* with Olivia de Havilland and Montgomery Clift). The heroine's mother died while giving birth to her. Her father, the wealthy physician who also delivered her, never forgives Catherine for being born (it is easier to blame his daughter than to blame himself for the death of his young wife). Catherine grows up clumsy, shy, and plain. She adores her father and keeps trying to win his love, to no avail.

Eventually, Catherine is courted by a handsome and ambitious but impoverished suitor named Morris Townsend. She falls deeply in love and gains new self-confidence from her suitor's adoration. But Catherine's father, convinced that Townsend is attracted only to Catherine's inheritance (for what else could he see in her?), refuses to consent to their marriage. He further tells Catherine that if she marries against his wishes, he will cut off her inheritance. Catherine would still have a healthy income from her dead mother's trust (Catherine's father had also married into a rich family—it takes a fortune hunter to recognize another), but her mother's legacy is modest compared to what she'd inherit from her father.

Catherine cares nothing about the money—she's madly in love with Townsend and wants only to be his wife, but she can't bear the thought of alienating her father completely. Her lover also doesn't want to lose the fortune. They wait it out, hoping her father will come around, which he never does. Eventually, Townsend abandons Catherine when it's clear that she won't get her father's money—

breaking her heart and delighting her father, who has been proven right, even at the cost of destroying Catherine's happiness. In addition to losing her lover, Catherine also loses her love for her father, once she fully confronts the truth that the father she adored has never really liked her one bit.

Other men, nicer men, ask Catherine to marry—but she refuses their proposals. Betrayed by her first love, she won't risk love again. But why would she give up on love, or the hope of being loved, after one disappointment? Most people recover from a romantic rejection, so why not Catherine?

As in Heathcliff's life, the real injury came before. Catherine was abandoned from the day she was born. From the start, her father, who was her entire life, had made her feel unlovable and unworthy of love. He also made her feel responsible for her mother's death. When Townsend professed his love, Catherine gained confidence for the first time, but his betrayal only confirmed what her father had taught her: that she didn't deserve to be loved or to be happy. One romantic rejection was enough to confirm the formative losses and to keep her from ever risking love again.

Catherine's father also transmitted the message that she didn't have his permission to leave him. She already felt guilty for her mother's death, and though she came to hate her father for destroying her chance of happiness, she also could never leave him. She spent the rest of her life in his house—remaining there even after he died. This is actually a fairly common story, although the people who live inside it are rarely consciously aware of its source.

Catherine's suitor, Morris Townsend, appeared to be unlike her father, at least superficially. On closer inspection the two men were very much alike: ambitious and self-centered. Catherine needed a lover who could undo the damage inflicted by her father, but she found (or was found by) one who was actually his reincarnation and who sealed the original judgment that she was not lovable. Townsend wanted to separate from his past too, and he needed her father's money and approval for that end, even more than he needed Catherine's love.

If you can't recover from the betrayal of a first love, or the person you love blames all of his problems on the damage inflicted by his first marriage, you might look back further in your life or your partner's life to find the original source of the problem.

When Partners Die and You Can't Let Them Go

The guilt over leaving one's parents—by either becoming independent or choosing a love they don't approve of—can last a lifetime. In fact, many widows and widowers feel prohibited from loving again until they decide their departed partners would have given their permission or blessing to the new union. The dead spouse has now, unconsciously, taken the place of the parent, or has become a parental surrogate. From their heavenly position, they hold or withhold their permission for the survivor to fall in love again. The survivor would like to make a new life but feels guilty about leaving the former beloved behind—his current self-reproach echoes with his childhood guilt about moving away from his parents. In this case, the guilt may be felt more consciously because the new love is only possible because the parental surrogate has actually died.

The need for parental permission is still there but is now expressed as the survivor's refusal to give up the lost one in favor of a new love. If the survivor falls in love with someone very different from his first partner—someone who pleases him in a way his first partner could not, or someone who draws him into a new world of experience—it makes him feel even more guilty, because it seems to leave his first love further behind. It also resonates with his childhood guilt over moving away from his parents.

Sometimes he looks for signs that his late spouse would have approved of this match for him and would have wanted him to move on. But some people are too guilty to allow themselves a new and different pleasure, or to ever truly be in love again. Instead they marry someone who won't make them happy or someone who won't ever threaten the primacy of the first love.

The recent movie *Return to Me* explores this dilemma of needing permission to move on from a lover who died. Bob is a young architect who is madly in love with his wife, Elizabeth. She is killed in an automobile accident, and he can't stop grieving. At the time of her death, he'd consented to donate her heart to an anonymous recipient.

The heart goes to a young woman, Grace, who has never had a lover because she was always too sick (before the transplant) to live a normal life. A year later, Bob and Grace meet when he comes to the family restaurant where she works. They both fall in love at first sight. Only later does Grace recognize that the heart she received came from Bob's late wife. The revelation threatens their love, because it arouses deeper guilt for Bob about Elizabeth and it also insures her permanent presence. How could he ever make love to Grace, seeing the surgical scar on her chest, without feeling Elizabeth is there?

Eventually he resolves his dilemma by believing this was all part of a greater plan and what Elizabeth obviously wanted. It was her way of living on with him after she died. He can love Grace without leaving Elizabeth behind. Although such an event could not happen in real life, it does reflect the love story repeated by people whose parents made them feel guilty about separating: a story that makes love forbidden because, unconsciously, you believe that love has killed or will kill your parent.

Some couples enter into a second marriage precisely because it won't require either one to give up their attachment to their lost partners. Fran and Howard met and married in late middle age, shortly after they were both widowed. Although they were drawn to each other, the real bond in their marriage was built around sharing their grief over losing the first and real loves of their lives. In this marriage, there have always been four partners. The ghosts of their first loves are always hovering over the pair. They constantly remind each other and outsiders that their first loves will always be the most important one.

Instead of moving into a house they chose and furnished together, Fran and Howard held on to the houses they had built and shared with their first spouses. They used one, in the city, during weekdays, and the other, by the shore, during weekends and the summer. The tacit agreement of this marriage was that neither would ever have to stop giving first place to their first loves. But even beyond the pain of feeling they have lost their only soul mates, it also hurts the couple to recognize that they will never be their partner's most important love. As a result, like the hero of the movie *Chasing Amy*, they constantly try to even the score, reminding each other they will never measure up to the lost partner.

Not a day goes by without several references to the lost loves. Those first unions have been exalted, in memory, to a perfection that never existed in real life. In her book of essays, *Never Say Goodbye*, Phyllis Rose has observed that many of us appreciate life more when we look back at it, since memory works to highlight the best times and screen out what was dull and annoying.

There's no reason to erase the good memories of a partner who has died and no reason to burn every object connected to that person. If you are involved in a second love you need to ask yourself honestly what your priority is. Do you want to be more involved with the partner who is dead or the partner who is alive? Is your dead partner playing the role, in your unconscious mind, that your parent once did, withholding permission for you to leave them or be happy in love? Is your new partner relegating you to a secondary role, telling you you'll never take the place of his first love? The person who didn't have parental permission to leave in the first place will always struggle with guilt about being happy.

People need a reasonable time to grieve (and it is different for everyone), but if they (or you) go on talking constantly about the lost lover, it's time to impose some limits. Perhaps you might say: Do you want to be with me or with your dead wife? If you want to be with me, we need to live in our own home—not the one you shared with her. If you want to be with me, you can't talk about her all the time. If you or your partner can't stop yourself from reminiscing, and you decide you want to save your relationship, you may need to impose some rules. Put aside a time when such talk is allowed. You might agree that reminiscing about the lost ones is allowed only once a month, or one hour a week.

Sometimes only one member of a couple is in love with a dead first love. She might not ever speak of the missing one, and her spouse may be entirely ignorant of her grief. But the ghost of the dead secretly hangs over the marriage. James Joyce's novella *The Dead*, and its movie adaptation directed by the late John Huston, are moving renditions of this theme.

Ghosts

The setting is in Dublin in 1904. Gabriel Conroy and his wife, Gretta, have spent the evening at the annual Christmas gathering of relatives and friends who are all growing older. At the party, one of the guests sings a love song, and Gretta's husband can see that she is transfixed. Gabriel is aroused by desire for his wife and by all the emotions stirred up that evening—many of them resonating with loss. Next Christmas, he wonders, will all these people still be sitting around the table? It's likely that some of them will be gone.

It is snowing hard, and that night the couple stay in a hotel to avoid the long drive home. Gretta (played in the movie by Anjelica Huston) is remote and finally confesses to her husband that the song had moved her so deeply because it reminded her of a boy who loved her when she was seventeen, a boy named Michael Furey, who sang that song to her. He was frail and heartbroken when her parents arranged to send her away to convent school. The night before she was to leave, Michael Furey had stood outside her window all night, in the freezing winter rain, begging her not to leave. He caught a cold, and a week later he was dead.

Gretta weeps for her dead first love—she sobs as if Michael Furey had died that very night. As she tells her husband the story for the first time, Gabriel realizes that he has never felt the passion that Michael Furey felt for his wife when she was seventeen. He becomes aware of his emotional limitations—he would never die for love. For the first time, he also sees the depth of passion and loneliness buried within his wife that he'd never noticed in twenty years of marriage.

After Gretta falls asleep, Gabriel stands by the window and watches the snow that is silently covering the land. He thinks about the snow covering the grave of Michael Furey, and that one day it will cover his own. His usual preoccupations suddenly appear trivial, pondering the death we are all moving toward. Comparing the great, first, love of his wife, he realizes "how poor a part he, husband, had played in her life."

How could Gabriel have been with Gretta for twenty years and not have known what was buried in his wife's heart? Perhaps the pain of losing her first love led Gretta to choose a man who was not as passionate as Michael Furey. Gabriel was a self-absorbed man who would never notice his wife's reserve. She could not go through the pain of losing such a love again, or the pain of seeing someone die out of love for her. Gretta didn't need to speak constantly of her first love to achieve distance in her marriage, as Fran and Howard did. She chose a man who didn't even notice how much of her was locked away.

PART TWO: RECAPTURE

The Return to a First Love

Among the middle-aged, widowed, and divorced, there is a common fantasy of finding and marrying one's long-lost first love. At its core, the wish to return to our first love, or the person we loved from a distance, is really about turning back the clock and recapturing all the good things we remember from our youth. When we dream about finding our first love, we want to erase the disappointments we encountered, and return to a time of innocence and hope—before we made major errors, and before life's knocks made us cynical or disillusioned. Many people think of their first love as their purest love—when they were most open and free of calculation. Sometimes a person who gave up her true love because of parental objections finally feels free enough in middle age to pursue what she really wanted. People still go to their high school or college reunions to find the love of their youth, or they do their search on the Internet. Surprisingly, these reunions often work out, and some couples who have been separated for decades live happily ever after. But why is this such an appealing fantasy?

Sometimes, we wish to undo big mistakes—and refinding a first love gives us what we failed to get before. For example, when Karen O'Conner was a young woman, she wanted to get away from her controlling parents and her life in suburban New Jersey. She passed up marrying her first love—her high school sweetheart—because she thought he wasn't strong enough or ambitious enough to get the two of them away from her parents and away from the world where she grew up.

Instead, she married a successful lawyer, who did indeed carry her away. But he tried to control her even more than her parents did. She had managed to get away from home, but she was even more unhappy than before. Many years later she divorced her husband and looked up her high school sweetheart. He was still living in the general area where Karen had grown up. He was divorced himself, and they fell in love again. They made a very happy marriage twenty years after she first turned him down. What made her so happy?

Recovering Your Self

After Karen's divorce from her controlling first husband, she felt that she had lost her past. We all wish to feel some continuity in life, and when we divorce a partner who has shared a big chunk of it, that leaves a huge hole that yearns to be filled. We don't miss the person as much as we miss the continuity in our identity.

When Karen married her high school boyfriend, she filled in that hole—she was able to join her lost past and lost youth with the woman she is today. Even going back to the place where she grew up was very comforting—it restored many nice things about her childhood, but her parents were no longer controlling, and neither was her second husband. An old love can do this—bring back the best part of one's youth, an idealized past, without the parental interference. It's the best of both worlds.

To recover that feeling of continuity, you don't need an actual lover from your youth. Anyone who has some connection to your past can fill the hole. An old friend or acquaintance, or even someone you didn't know at that time but who grew up in the same environment, may help you rediscover your past.

The need that is filled this way resembles that of people who never got along with their controlling parents but who later cherish the furniture or objects they inherit from their parents. These things provide a sense of continuity with their youth and parental protection without the frustrating reality of their parents' actual presence.

Beyond a sense of continuity, we want our first love to restore us to youth. Even though our first loves have grown older, as we have, they still remember us—and see us—the way we were, when we were young and untarnished by age and the disappointments of life. Through our reflection in their eyes, we hope to recapture our innocent self, when all of life stretched out before us.

The Way We Were

The movie *The Way We Were* taps into this common nostalgic fantasy. Barbra Streisand and Robert Redford portray opposites. (She's a Jewish political activist; he's the WASP golden boy who takes the path of least resistance.) They meet in college and later marry. They try, unsuccessfully, to bridge the gap between them, but eventually they divorce. Years later, they run into each other in front of the Plaza Hotel in New York, and we see they have reverted to their original types.

She is handing out political pamphlets, and he has an elegant blonde woman on his arm. They look at each other, and we know they are remembering the love they once had, and all that might have been. He could never live up to the idealized view she held of him, but seeing her reminds him of his youthful ambitions to be a serious writer—ambitions she had encouraged and that he ultimately rejected. Having a lover who remembers us in our youth, when we were innocent and full of hope, is also one of the great pleasures of marrying one's first love, and part of the grief of losing them.

In Sue Miller's recent novel, *While I Was Gone,* the heroine, Jo Becker, has been happily married for almost thirty years but is suffering from an empty nest. All of her three daughters have moved away from home and are living independently—lives in which she is not the central figure. Jo loves her husband, but she feels a sense of emptiness and loss. Also, her life has become predictable and she's starting to feel the dread of aging and death. She misses the feeling of total open-endedness she had at one point in her youth—the feeling that she could be anything she wanted.

Then one day, a man Jo had lived with back in the 1960s, during a critical time in her youth (he wasn't her lover, but they had shared rooms in a commune) suddenly reappears by chance. She falls in love with Eli, even though he is irritating and lacks the qualities she loves in her husband. She falls in love even though she intellectually understands her feelings have less to do with Eli than with yearning for her lost youthful self. Eli represents a connection to herself when she was young. Jo realizes this "self-intoxication" is often misperceived as love for someone else.

But that self-intoxication can't be lightly dismissed. It's exactly what we are looking for in romantic love—someone who boosts our own self-regard. And in real life, the recapture of an old love may turn out to be a wonderful miracle.

The Reunited

Many years ago, Phil Donahue devoted an hour-long television program to the stories of four couples who had been high school sweethearts and who'd been parted, for different reasons, for up to thirty-odd years. Finally they found each other later in life and fell in love again, and married happily. Their stories reflect very common experiences and teach us a great deal about first loves.

Donahue opened the show by posing a common fantasy to his studio audience: "There's a guy that was in your life who kissed you good night. You'll never forget him and you'd love to meet him again. The fantasy comes true on our program."

The first couple, Glen and Andree, were from the Midwest. As far back as grade school they had planned to marry each other, but it took them thirty-two years to make it to the altar. Why? When Glen was eighteen and Andree was sixteen, he'd given her an engagement ring. But Glen's grandmother (his caretaker), a very pious Lutheran, objected to the marriage because Andree was of a different religious faith. Unable to challenge his grandmother he asked Andree to give the ring back, and devastated, he joined the marines. That was in 1956—thirty-two years before the show was aired in 1988.

After the engagement was broken off, both of them married and divorced other people. They each had three children in their first marriages. Andree was divorced in 1972 and never expected to marry again. When she was asked if she had ever thought about Glen during those years, she denied it: "You don't think about something you lost and think you will never get back."

But Glen thought about her, after he divorced four years earlier. He went back to the small town where they had been children and found the woman who had been Andree's stepmother. She gave him Andree's telephone number. He called her, and Andree recalls that when she heard his voice, "My little heart hurt." He flew to the town where she was living, and she went to pick him up at the airport. When he saw her, he just dropped his bags where he stood, and they embraced. It was as if they had never been apart. They got married a few weeks later, on Valentine's Day.

Couple two, Dick and Barbara, also from the Midwest, were in their midforties. They had been sweethearts since grammar school, but Barbara had always known that when she graduated from high school she was going to enter a convent—which she did. Dick asked her if she was going to stay in the convent forever, and Barbara said, yes, absolutely. So twenty-eight years ago he thought he had lost her forever.

A few years after their relationship ended Dick married someone else, and on the second day of his marriage, he brought his new wife to the convent where Barbara was now living as Sister Colette. Dick had needed to see her in her full nun habit to know his relationship with her was really over. After they visited in the parlor for an hour, they all went to the chapel and prayed, and Barbara felt they had gone their separate ways and this was meant to be. She didn't think about him anymore.

After eleven years in the convent, Barbara decided she wanted to leave. She moved to a different city, but from time to time she'd visit her hometown and would see Dick and his wife and their three children.

A few years later her phone rang. The man called her Barbara, and she asked "Who is this?" Everyone else called her Colette. He said, "Don't tell me you haven't recognized my voice." He told her he was coming to see her, and she knew in that instant that Dick was getting a divorce, and that her life was about to change.

They were 150 miles apart. He got in his car and drove to her immediately. Two years later, when Dick's first marriage was annulled, they were finally married. That was ten years earlier, and since then, Barbara has become a close stepmother to Dick's three children.

One would have thought the Donahue audience would be moved by these tales of love recovered after decades of separation. In fact, most people who responded from the audience sounded hostile and skeptical. It seemed that many of the women in the audience had been left by their husbands, or had mothers who had been abandoned by their fathers who made happy second marriages while their mothers never did. Almost all of the audience identified with the absent first wife—and asked pointed questions of the couples such as "Did she contribute to the breakup of your marriage?" "Did you think about her when you were being intimate with your wife all those years?" "Since most of you have been divorced before, aren't you fearful that this won't work out either?" One angry audience member even attacked the host. "How about you, Phil? Do you have an ex-sweetheart, and does Marlo know?"

A surprised Phil Donahue tried to figure out what was angering them. "I see, it's bad enough that he got divorced, but it's worse that he married his high school sweetheart." The audience members, almost all women, explained that it was worse that he returned to an earlier girlfriend, because that seemed to nullify his first marriage even more than just the divorce. Their reaction should serve as a useful reminder: if you find yourself wildly happy in love, don't expect everyone around you to celebrate—especially those who have been romantically hurt.

Undoing Mistakes

These stories of reunion are not so unusual—one hears about them all the time. And the elements are common: although they were in love in their youth, religious differences, race, class or ethnic differences, age differences, or their parents made them part. They went their separate ways and the choices and commitments they made eventually unraveled. When they meet again, their circumstances have changed.

When Parents Break Up First Loves

For example, Sharon Cohen grew up in a Jewish, middle-class family in Pennsylvania. In high school she fell madly in love with Bobby, a classmate from a Catholic, Italian family. They wanted to marry, but Sharon's parents objected strenuously to the match and sent her off to college. Eventually she married a Jewish doctor, exactly the kind of husband her parents hoped she would marry. Sharon had three children and led a comfortable life, but her marriage was never that happy, and her husband was increasingly remote. He worked all the time and was rarely home. When her children were teenagers she confronted what she'd suspected all along—he'd been having affairs for many years. They divorced, and Sharon returned to work as a nurse. As her children left home for college, one by one, Sharon thought about Bobby more and more, and imagined what her life would have been like if she had married her first love.

One day, on an impulse, she called her high school alumni contact and got Bobby's current phone number. He was married and living a hundred miles away. After hesitating for a few days she called him. It had been twenty years since they last spoke to each other. Bobby suggested they meet for lunch in a town halfway between their homes. It was a diner with comfortable booths, and sitting across from each other, they felt as they did when they were dating in high school. Twenty years just dropped away. Bobby told her he was unhappy in his marriage, although he had always been faithful to his wife. They met a few more times and realized they still loved each other and were right for each other. After Bobby obtained a divorce, the couple married, and the two are extremely happy.

Or consider Jim Turner. He was very bright but short and overweight in high school, definitely not one of the popular boys. In high school, Jim could only dream about his first crush, Eleanor, the beautiful girl who would never have looked at him twice, even if he'd had the nerve to ask. She married the captain of the football team. Jim became a brilliant businessman, earning millions of dollars and leading an interesting life, except that his marriage, made during college, had never made him happy.

Once he reached his fifties, he began to think about Eleanor. He wondered how her life had turned out. At fifty-five Jim now had the self-confidence he'd never thought possible when he was a sixteen-year-old nerd. He did some research and found out Eleanor was still living near the town where they grew up. He called her and learned she was divorced and unattached. They met—she fell in love with him instantly, and his old desire for her was immediately rekindled. Jim divorced his wife and married Eleanor, and the two of them were deliriously happy. Jim's life was filled with joy for the first time in his life. Unfortunately, he died of a heart attack just a year after their marriage, but at least he found great happiness before he died.

Sometimes, the differences or obstacles that keep us from our first loves fall away with the passing years. Parents no longer control our lives. The disparities in physical beauty or social status or popularity are altered as life changes our circumstances. We regard ourselves differently, and the qualities we look for in a partner are different from those that mattered in our youth. So someone like Jim has a chance to go back and win the love of a girl who was beyond his reach when he was young. A victory like this can erase all the years of pain that come from making compromises based on low self-esteem.

Behind the Yearning

When first love is recaptured, it can be magically wonderful. It can wipe away years of disappointment and boredom, and hopes that didn't come true. When we meet again with our first loves, we can recover the passions and dreams of youth and add the maturity and wisdom that come with age. But we can't always marry or get back together with our first loves, so people who yearn for the person they loved in their youth need to recognize what they are really looking for: something they had in youth and lost in themselves. The sense of openness to life, the uncompromising passion, the willingness to take risks, to lay everything on the line, the thrill of adventure and forging into unknown territory, the faith in good things that lie ahead.

All of these feelings can be recovered in other ways, when recapturing a long-lost love isn't possible. There are many ways to find and explore new interests, or to get involved in exciting new adventures. When you find yourself pining for an old love it's a signal that something is missing in your life, but you need to figure out exactly what it is and remember there's more than one way of finding it.

Bringing Love Back to Life

Obviously, people who marry their first loves in youth sometimes lose the person they fell in love with, even if they stay together. The qualities that first drew them together often seem to disappear, and sometimes they can't even be remembered. Couples like this often wonder what they saw in each other—they can't even conjure up an image of the person they fell in love with so long ago. But sometimes the person you fell in love with can be recovered. The movie *Peggy Sue Got Married* reminds us those youthful and appealing qualities may still lie buried beneath all the anger and disappointment that have accumulated over the years.

In the 1986 movie, forty-two-year-old Peggy Sue (Kathleen

Turner) is divorcing her husband Charlie (her first love) after twenty-five years of marriage. She decides to go to her twenty-fifth high school reunion. Called up to the stage to be crowned for her beauty and loveliness, which remain, her heart suddenly stops and she passes out.

When she awakes she finds herself in the year 1958—in her teenage body and surrounded by the friends and family of her youth, but with the mind and knowledge of her forty-two-year-old self.

Many of us wish we could travel back in time, to spend an hour or a day with those we loved who are no longer with us, with the wisdom we have gained in the years that have passed. We would tell them how much we loved them, and we could act with the knowledge of hindsight. That wish is granted to Peggy Sue, who is seventeen once more, with her family and friends, and being courted by the boy (played by Nicolas Cage) she knows she'll eventually marry and divorce.

She could change the course of her future and make a different choice. But she would miss her children, and not having them would be unthinkable. In addition, she gets another chance to see the qualities she once loved in Charlie—his devotion to her, his sweetness, his passion for music and dreams of becoming a singer. In her middle-aged anger over his infidelity and his failures, she'd forgotten that he also once had dreams that he'd been forced to give up when she became pregnant. These are the qualities that made her fall in love with him when she was seventeen. When she awakes in a hospital room, Charlie is there, and they reconcile with a love that has been reawakened.

We can't always bring love back to life, or reunite with the person we loved when we were young. But often we are really missing what our first loves represent—the idealism, honesty, excitement, and hopefulness of youth, as well as the courage to take risks, the fun of adventures with friends, and the joy of being alive. I have even heard college students express deep nostalgia and longing for the first loves they had in high school or junior high school. They are not yet twenty years old but already, some of them feel old and cynical. They are further proof that feeling young or old is not just a matter of chronological time. Until the day we die, we have the power to restore many of the feelings of youth that brought us such joy, whether or not we can actually recapture our first love.

SELF-REFLECTIONS

1. Do you feel you hurt your parents when you asserted your independence or happiness apart from them? Did they give you the message that separating from them would harm them?

2. If your partner died, are you blaming your new partner or potential new partners for not being the person you lost? Are you open to seeing their own good qualities, even if they are different from those of your lost partner? Do you feel guilty about loving someone new because you think it would have hurt the partner who died? Who can give you permission to love someone new?

3. If you have fantasies about reuniting with an old love, have you thought about what this might mean? Did you give up the chance to be with someone who is right for you, and do you think he might feel the same way? If the answers are yes, what is stopping you from calling him? Or do you think you are missing something about your self or the life you had long ago, when you knew this person? If you can't reunite with your old love, is there another way to recapture what you miss from your youth?

CHAPTER TWO

❦

Pygmalion:
The Mentor and the Protégée

For the young man is handsome, but the old man is great.

—VICTOR HUGO, "Booz endormi"

Most of us know the *Pygmalion* story from its musical adaptation, *My Fair Lady*. In Greek mythology, Pygmalion was a sculptor who fell in love with the beautiful statue he created from a lump of clay. He was incapable of loving a real woman. His only love was for a statue that displayed his own brilliance.

Most Pygmalion stories, including the movies *Educating Rita* and *Annie Hall*, have focused on the character of the male hero—on his narcissism and inability to love. This is also the portrait of Henry Higgins (Rex Harrison), the phonetics professor in *My Fair Lady*. On a bet, he sets out to prove he can transform Eliza Doolittle (an unwashed "guttersnipe" who lives on the streets, sellings flowers—played by Audrey Hepburn) into a woman who could pass as royalty. He cares nothing about the woman he's reconstructing—once he has demonstrated his genius, he forgets all about her. It's only when she leaves him that he notices she was more than the sum of the parts he gave to her. This is the classic Pygmalion scenario.

But what about the woman in this familiar love story? What does she really want? Can there be a happy ending to a love story between a teacher and student, between two people who started out as distinctly unequal?

Many young women fall in love with an admired teacher and mentor, or a worldly, cultivated older man. He's more powerful than she, and that is part of his attraction. But the protégée doesn't want to be dominated forever, or to spend her whole life admiring her teacher. She has great ambitions of her own, and an independent spirit. She falls in love with a man who has the skills to develop her own talent and potential. She admires him, and most of all, she wants to learn from him—to gain his skills or knowledge for herself.

The protégée's motives and needs are complex, but she's usually not just looking for lessons. Most often, her ambitions and her desire to learn from her mentor are deeply entwined with her need to be recognized and nurtured by a parental figure—someone who thinks she is worth the time and effort of instruction. She is looking for the attention and help that her own parents never gave her. In some cases, her needs for recognition and nurture are her deepest, though unconscious, motivations—she becomes a brilliant student, primarily in order to win the love of her teacher. But there is also a fiercely competitive strain in her—she wants to prove that she is the best.

Just being the chosen student—merely attracting the interest of an admired teacher or a distinguished older man—in itself shows the world that she is special. Often this woman falls in love with her mentor because he recognizes her potential.

But for the most competitive protégée, that's not enough. Once she's extracted everything her mentor has to offer she may leave him behind for an even bigger mentor, or take over his position. At the other extreme, many protégées wind up with broken hearts when they realize their teachers aren't gods but merely narcissists with feet of clay. Despite all the problems I've mentioned, this kind of relationship can also turn out very well—into a long and happy love, especially when it evolves into an equal partnership.

The Pygmalion story has a natural history, and a variety of characteristic dangers and rewards. Initially, the woman's interest might not be sexual—usually, the couple first meet as a mentor and advisee, or a teacher and student.

In the corporate world, there is probably less mentoring than there used to be. This is probably the result of increased competition and the devaluation of older employees, which has altered the relation between generations. But young people still hope to find a wise parental figure who can show them the ropes. Many women who work in the financial markets, for example, wish they had a strong male mentor—a benevolent figure who takes them seriously. They don't want a mentor who is competitive or indifferent (as many young women assume a senior female mentor would be).

The protégée often expects that she will get more help from a male mentor for two reasons. First, she assumes an older man will feel less competitive toward her, which isn't necessarily true, because both men and women can feel competitive toward a junior colleague. Her assumption that older women would compete with her may stem from her own projection of competitive feelings toward senior women. Second, she thinks an older man is more likely to be flattered by her admiration, and less likely to notice her faults. She's probably right. The man who is aging and doesn't get much admiration at home is naturally drawn to an attractive young woman who thinks he is brilliant. That's why so many men who are otherwise cautious will risk their professional careers to have affairs with forbidden, younger employees.

The mentor-protégée relationship typically changes when the man reveals he's fallen in love. Usually he's older, and the protégée's admiration is gratifying and something he's probably not received from his wife or his children for a very long time. The protégée's adoration boosts his self-esteem, and his power to help her makes him feel stronger. Whether or not this will turn into a lasting and mutually gratifying love depends on the questions of competition, on whose needs are being served, and on whether it can evolve into an equal relationship.

One big question always is: Can the mentor appreciate the younger woman's qualities and achievements that are independent of him? Or, is he only interested in being admired for what he has taught her? Can he tolerate her growing independence and her widening circle of friends—the fact that her world and her opportunities have expanded, partly because of him—or does he need her to worship him, exclusively? Can he take her seriously as a partner, or will he cut her loose once the affair has made him feel better about himself and proven that he's still attractive to young women? If his colleagues frown on the relationship, will their opinion mean more to him than the protégée's love?

For her part, the real question is: Does she really love him, or does she just love what he can give her? Is she ready to dispose of him and move up the ladder of mentors after he's taught her what he knows? Once he's shown her the ropes, would she rather take over his job and have adoring assistants herself?

These are the tough questions that both lovers must face when asking themselves whether their relationship will work.

Consider the story of Vicki Lewis. Fresh out of college, Vicki wanted to become an expert in the stock market. She was very bright and ambitious, but she had absolutely no self-confidence. When Vicki heard that the manager of a big mutual fund was looking for young analysts (and interviewing them personally) she immediately applied for the job. This financial wizard was well known and had appeared frequently in the news, so Vicki already knew about him. She was twenty-one and he was thirty-eight, nearly old enough to be her father. An older cousin of Vicki's who also worked in the market told Vicki that Robert Lieff was very sexy and recently divorced, and that hundreds of women were chasing after him. She thought it would be great for Vicki if she could land the job, but she didn't think her young cousin had much of a chance competing against applicants who had a lot more experience.

When Vicki walked into the interview, Robert Lieff said hello and then they talked for the next two hours. He was very interested in her ideas, and she couldn't believe how much time he was spending with her. At one point, he called his secretary and told her to put off his calls. Then he told Vicki that this had been an amazing conversation, and he wanted to see her again, soon—the next day, if it were possible. He had engagements all day but would try to cancel them. Vicki was totally smitten by the time he called her the next morning.

They met in his office at three and talked for the next several hours, into the evening. As it grew dark, he ordered sandwiches and coffee. At some point, he fell silent, and Vicki was stunned when he reached over and took her hand. Only three weeks later he told her he was serious about her, and he didn't want her to date anyone else.

Vicki was totally blown away by this declaration. All she could think to say was, "This is so much to think about," but she said it in a way that was encouraging. He answered protectively, "It must feel like I'm rushing you. Take as long as you want."

Within months, they were married. She was madly in love with him. He knew so much about so many things that Vicki wanted to know. She had grand ambitions, but she didn't think she could get anywhere on just her own power. Attached to Robert, she now hoped his knowledge and skill might rub off on her. Even after they were married, she worshipped him. She felt that a prince had come through with the glass slipper, and she kept asking herself, in disbelief, "Me? You want me?"

There was however one element in their relationship that made Vicki uneasy from the start. She was frightened by the intensity of Robert's need for her. His tremendous involvement with her had made her feel flattered at first, but almost immediately, it made her feel nervous and guilty. Vicki had always had trouble turning away from someone's neediness—it pulled her in like an overwhelming magnetic force. So she wasn't able to distance herself from his constant demands for attention. He had few close friends and relied on her exclusively for all his emotional needs. As a couple, they spent all their time doing the things that interested Robert. Despite her nagging misgivings, she went ahead with the marriage to Robert because she couldn't let him down, and also because she desperately wanted to get away from her mother.

Vicki's father had been seriously ill when she was a child and died when she was in the eighth grade. Her mother had become very needy and dependent on Vicki, living her life through her daughter and controlling her with guilt. Robert's father had also died when he was a young child, and Vicki had learned as a child that people like her mother and Robert just needed protection, and she'd been raised to provide it. So in trying to get away from her mother, she had married a new version of her mother.

Once Robert's need for constant attention became increasingly evident, he no longer seemed like the god he once appeared to be. He was like her, which she defined as unworthy of admiration. And her plan to gain Robert's knowledge about the stock market never went very far. Most of their relationship was devoted to his problems and needs. Three years after they were married, she was able to overcome tremendous guilt and fear about deserting him and moved out.

Initially, Vicki had been drawn to this union because she was playing out the Pygmalion story. When none of her needs were being met and the relationship evolved into a story of Rescue (with Vicki as the rescuer), she was turned off because Robert was too strongly reminiscent of her mother. His need to be admired and also his need to have his opinions and tastes prevail in everything they did and talked about left little room for Vicki's development.

At first she would memorize every word of wisdom that came from his lips, but eventually he seemed like a didactic bore. Still, the relationship was not a total disaster. Vicki got out before the relationship became mean, and it served its purpose in moving her away from her mother. Robert had never mocked her ambitions or made her feel inadequate, so he didn't tear down her self-esteem. But ultimately, he cared more about having an adoring audience than in helping Vicki move ahead with her own life.

Both Vicki and Robert had been looking for the fantasy of perfect protection, and when one of them, Vicki, didn't find it in the relationship, she needed for it to end. Robert was shocked when he learned that Vicki had been unhappy. His need for the all-protective mother figure that he imagined she was had blinded him from seeing her real feelings. For Vicki, Robert first appeared as a powerful, omniscient parent but wound up becoming the child.

The marriage was clearly a mistake, but each partner grew from it. Both Vicki and Robert became more independent as a result of acknowledging the flaws in their relationship, and each went on to more successful marriages. Vicki also created a successful business.

Their story reminds us that members of a couple are usually living out different plots. Vicki was in a Pygmalion fantasy, so she expected Robert to spend time instructing her. But after their engagement he was less fascinated by her potential than eager to have an adoring audience. Robert was hoping for someone to rescue him from his depression, although it took a while for Vicki to see she was doing more parenting in their relationship. People always get into trouble when they don't look objectively at their partners and ask what story their partner is living in. They get into trouble when they block out the warning signs, as Vicki did, and deny the aspects of their lover's behavior that make them uneasy.

The popular 1988 movie *Working Girl* is another version of the Pygmalion plot. Melanie Griffith stars as Tess, the bright but innocent working-class secretary with big hair who travels from Staten Island to her job on Wall Street, where she dreams of becoming one of the traders. She hopes to be mentored by one of her male bosses, but all she ever gets is crude sexual harassment.

Finally, Tess is relieved when she's transferred to a beautiful female boss (Sigourney Weaver). At last, she believes, she's found the perfect mentor—a boss who will take her seriously, teach her, and treat her as an equal. At first, things look promising. Weaver shows her how to dress, speak, and act like a financial executive. She's full of tips about how to get ahead. But when Weaver is out of the office for a few weeks, after a skiing accident, Tess discovers that her female mentor has stolen her own brilliant idea for a financial acquisition, and that Weaver was planning to present it as her own. This betrayal sets Tess into action, using everything she has learned from her mentor. While her boss is away, she takes over her boss's office, home, and wardrobe. She assumes an identity that allows her to pull off the major deal that Weaver was about to steal from her. Even better, her boss's terrific boyfriend (played by Harrison Ford), a high-powered but honest trader, becomes Tess's advisor and partner in this venture, and they fall in love. He is the perfect mentor: he is generous and loving, and he wants her to shine. In the end, she displaces her female mentor in work and in love.

Perhaps this story of teacher and protégée could end happily because there's a good mentor and a wicked one: all of Melanie Griffith's competitiveness can be vented against her female boss, while her good male mentor may remain the perfect lover. As a mentor, Harrison Ford's character is the antithesis of Weaver's: he's honest and respectful of Griffith, and he also treats her as an equal and doesn't even take advantage of her sexually when he has the chance. He admires her spunk and courage, and he risks his own position when all those in power temporarily turn against her. They wind up in a loving relationship of equals, a balance they established from the start.

This movie speaks volumes about how many women feel (rightly or wrongly) about their female bosses, and explains why so many women become romantically involved with their male bosses and teachers. If movies reflect our fantasies and fears—and certainly they do—then movies about love between teachers and protégées may teach us what motivates this love scenario.

In large institutional settings, the mentor/protégé relationship has changed with the growing competition and instability at work. In a culture that believes the young represent the future and that wisdom and experience count for little, the older generation resents being devalued in the workplace. Older employees understandably are not that interested in helping people half their age who openly treat them as obsolete.

But even if the young think the old are obsolete, they still feel the need for mentors—someone to teach them the ropes in the business. Many young people are also still searching for something more personal—attention, approval, and wisdom from a parent surrogate, encouragement or practical help they never received from their own parents. They want a mentor who won't compete with them—someone who will put their needs and interests at the center of attention.

Here we see some interesting differences in the way our culture depicts mentor-protégé relationships between members of the same sex. In general, the male bonds between generations are greatly idealized—in movies like *Saving Private Ryan, An Officer and a Gentleman,* and *Wonder Boys,* the older males are perfectly unselfish father surrogates. In *Saving Private Ryan,* the sergeant literally sacrifices his life so the younger man may live, and Private Ryan spends the rest of his life trying to be worthy of his teacher.

The older man is portrayed as beyond needing to compete. In *Wonder Boys,* the college professor played by Mike Douglas shows no resentment when the college student he's been protecting steals his editor and gets a book contract that Douglas had long been working for. Moreover, Douglas just smiles when he learns his student's novel is actually an unflattering portrait of him! He's forgiving and amused because he's moved beyond competitiveness and youthful ambitions.

In contrast, our movies and novels about female mentors and students generally portray a vicious catfight—and always a ruthless betrayal of one of the women by the other. In *Working Girl*, it's the female boss who betrays first, legitimizing the revenge of the female protégée. In most of these stories, it's the younger woman who cannibalizes her female teacher—first extracting everything she might learn from her, then deposing her by stealing her job and often her lover.

In reality, men and women may be good or bad mentors to their protégés of either sex. It always depends on the individuals. But our popular culture obviously reflects widespread fantasies that influence the perceptions and choices of young people seeking teachers and mentors. The tremendous idealization of male mentors may stem from a childhood wish for a loving and attentive father, a desire that is never extinguished. Perhaps the unflattering portraits of female mentors spring from the general devaluation of older women, or the fact that most people are cared for by women when they are children and have more difficulty relating to maternal figures when they are seeking adult independence. In any case, stories between female mentors and protégées depicting fierce rivalries and betrayals are important to examine because of what they reveal about our deepest wishes and fears.

In the movies, the scheming competitiveness of the female protégée is usually fully displayed only when the mentor is female. The classic movie about this theme is the 1950 Academy Award winner, *All About Eve*, starring Bette Davis. Davis plays the role of a middle-aged star of the theater—a great actress named Margo Channing. She is anxious about aging for two reasons: she's becoming too old for the female leading roles, and she's afraid of losing her younger husband (who is also her writer-director). An adoring young fan, named Eve, approaches Margo and asks to work as her assistant. Margo takes in the protégée, who appears, at first, to worship her, but Eve is actually scheming to replace her—not only onstage but also in her marriage. When Margo tries to warn her husband, he accuses her of being paranoid.

In the end, the protégée does usurp her mentor's position

onstage, but her conniving behavior only brings Margo and her husband into a happier union while Eve becomes universally despised in her profession. In this story, the mentor gains wisdom and maturity from the betrayal by her protégée: like the professor of *Wonder Boys* she learns there is more to life than work, and that a career will only take you so far.

Collected Stories, a play by Donald Margulies, gives a contemporary twist on the Pygmalion story. The playwright has said that he was inspired by the plagiarism lawsuit between the novelist David Leavitt and the poet Stephen Spender. Spender claimed that words from Leavitt's novel had been lifted from his own memoir. Ultimately, Leavitt's novel was withdrawn from publication.

Margulies recast the story into a play about the relationship between a renowned fiction writer, Ruth Steiner, and her young, ambitious assistant Lisa Morrison, who aspires to be a writer. The older woman, who has never had a child, lavishes her time and energy on her, helping Lisa learn how to write. She also progressively opens her life to the young woman. After snooping in her mentor's books, Lisa discovers the suggestion of an old love affair between Ruth and a famous writer (now long dead). Seduced by her protégée's admiration and interest, and thinking of her as the daughter she never had, Ruth tells Lisa what she'd never revealed or written—the story of the great love of her life. Although Ruth has always counseled Lisa that writers can't be timid about using their own lives and the lives of others as grist for their work, she clearly had drawn the line when it came to this part of her life.

Lisa is eager to learn about her mentor's love affair, which Ruth recalls in poetic detail. Predictably, when Lisa needs material for a commercially successful novel, she publishes Ruth's personal love story, nearly verbatim, as her own creation. For this terrible betrayal, she is richly rewarded—the novel brings her not only wealth but literary prizes and acclaim that far surpass the success of her mentor. And besides betraying and stealing from her mentor, she stops coming to visit her when Ruth becomes seriously ill. Unlike Eve, she could not try to steal her mentor's actual partner, but she does it symbolically, by stealing the story of that love and claiming it as her own.

Although the love that Ruth Steiner had felt for her protégée was more motherly than romantic, this play illuminates the deep issues of the Pygmalion love story. First, it is heavily modeled on the parent-child bond: the rising of the younger one as the older one declines; their often-competing emotional needs and interests; the pain of the mentor who must watch the protégée become increasingly independent of her, largely because of what she has given to her. Most Pygmalion stories finally revolve around the question of exploitation: is this an exploitative relationship in either direction? Is the mentor sucking the young blood from the protégée, and using her for his own needs and self-esteem, or is the protégée merely cannibalizing the mentor?

Collected Stories ends with the mentor's rage, rather than the bemused acceptance portrayed in *All About Eve* and *Wonder Boys*. Ruth does not go quietly into the night. She lets her protégée know what she thinks about her behavior. Lisa refuses to apologize. In fact, she claims to be surprised that Ruth doesn't take satisfaction in her protégée's success.

In real life, do protégées actually usurp their mentors' positions? Sometimes they do, even when their mentors are their lovers.

One example involved a senior executive of a major Hollywood studio—call him Tom Silver. He was a hard-nosed workaholic but always made time for an affair. He became romantically involved with Cindy, his female assistant. Eventually he divorced his wife and married the younger protégée. Now Cindy was given her own little fiefdom within the studio—she could produce a few films of her own. And she had her own protégées (one of whom wound up having an affair with her husband, Tom).

Cindy learned well from her mentor. She was just as competitive as Tom in her business dealings. Her productions were very successful, but she began to covet her husband's position. Everyone who worked in their company knew he was having an affair with a young assistant, so Cindy retaliated by openly expressing her wish to replace her husband as the head of the company. Eventually they divorced (Silver marrying the assistant), and Cindy was hired as a senior executive of a major rival studio. If she couldn't usurp her husband's position, she could try to defeat him by making the rival company more successful.

Why is there so much competition in this type of love story? Some degree of rivalry is present in all intimate relationships, if only because lovers each have their own needs that cry out to be met, needs that sometimes are competing. In Pygmalion relationships the competitive element is just more obvious, because this kind of story attracts people who tend to have large ambitions—the protégée who wants a dedicated coach while the mentor, by definition, is usually someone who has achieved a respected position. The rivalry also builds up because the needs of the protégée and mentor often conflict. They are drawn to each other, first of all, because of those needs: the mentor for an admiring audience, the protégée for nurture. But both of them can't be the center of attention at once.

Also, whenever one person achieves public glory—in part because of the tutelage or support of another—the one who is standing in the wings while the other is applauded is naturally a little resentful. The one who nurtured the other's achievements will feel unappreciated and afraid of being used or left. At the same time, the one who had the courage to pursue something big has laid herself on the line and taken big risks: if she had failed, the humiliation would have been all hers. She doesn't want to recall that she owes her success to someone who coached her from the sidelines.

In *My Fair Lady,* Henry Higgins wins his bet when he succeeds at transforming Eliza into a woman who passes as royalty at a ball. (Of course, it didn't hurt that Audrey Hepburn was the lump of clay he had to work with.) Returning from the grand ball, at which the beautiful Eliza drew much attention and danced with the prince, Henry Higgins bursts into an exultant song about his great achievement. While he celebrates his victory with his colleague and his staff, Eliza is left standing alone and forgotten. No one is thinking about all the hard work she had done to remake herself.

The Pygmalion relationship is found among all kinds of people, not just those who run corporations or bask in the limelight. I once attended an award ceremony for writers whose books had been selected for special prizes. One of the recipients had died a few months earlier, and his widow accepted his posthumous award. She spoke three times longer than any of the authors accepting prizes.

There were gasps in the audience when the widow unselfconsciously referred to the honored work as "my book." She went on to describe how she and her husband had toiled for years on the work, even as her husband couldn't lift himself from bed, in the terminal stages of his cancer. Her husband had been gravely ill throughout most of the writing, but she brought the material he needed to his bed, and together, they completed the work, line by line.

Surely, she believed she was offering a tribute to her husband, letting everyone know how much this work meant to him. But her speech came across as a tribute to herself—the handmaiden who finally got to take a bow—and she wasn't going to be rushed from the stage after all those years of waiting for recognition.

The Pygmalion relationship is also at the heart of most love affairs between young women and much older, distinguished men. The man may not be a mentor in a narrow, professional sense—but he may be broadening her horizons in a general way and teaching her about things she can't learn from books or school courses. She falls in love not just with the man, but with an entire world he's the center of, a world she could never comprehend without his guidance.

One of the most perceptive portraits of such a love appears in Diane Johnson's recent novel, *Le Divorce*. The narrator and heroine is Isabel Walker from Santa Barbara, California. She's a film school dropout who has been sent to Paris by her parents to help her older stepsister, Roxy, the more admired daughter. Roxy is married to a Parisian man from an upper-class French family and is pregnant with her second child. Isabel is supposed to babysit her three-year-old niece, but her parents also hope that living in Paris will motivate Isabel to mature and develop new interests.

As it turns out, Isabel's arrival coincides with the departure of Roxy's husband, Charles-Henri Persand. He has fallen in love with another woman and wants a divorce. While Roxy's status is rapidly falling, Isabel begins an affair with her brother-in-law's distinguished uncle—the most exalted Persand. Edgar is a handsome and influential political advisor who is almost seventy, roughly fifty years older than Isabel. For the first time, Isabel is winning the competition with her older sister. Isabel's married lover, *l'Oncle* Edgar, is important, a *personnage;* she has seen him on television, discussing world affairs.

As in most Pygmalion stories, the protégée gains a new view of herself when the mentor treats her with serious interest. Edgar takes Isabel to the finest Parisian restaurants and patiently instructs her, not only about French attitudes and manners, but also about sex. Edgar's lovemaking is inseparable from the larger sensual education he provides: the language, the cuisine, the style, the arts.

Under Edgar's tutelage, Isabel undergoes a remarkable transformation. On one occasion, they go to the opera (her first time), and between the acts they are greeted by a younger friend of Edgar's— the director of the French Ministry of Culture. When the director asks Isabel her opinion, she is thrilled that a man of his station would assume they could have such a conversation, and that she would have an opinion. She feels this is a major turning point in her life.

This is also a central theme in the Pygmalion story. The sexual attraction the young woman feels for her older lover is inseparable from all the knowledge he is imparting to her, and from the way she feels transformed by his interest in her. Isabel's story also illuminates another key feature of the Pygmalion plot. Initially, the heroine feels dependent on her lover for her new identity. But there comes a time when she realizes she has changed enough to hold her own in his world—usually when her lover's peers also find her interesting and worthy of attention, giving her independent confirmation.

When Edgar's family discovers the affair, he immediately informs Isabel that he is needed elsewhere to negotiate an important political settlement; they will have to end their amour. He tries to console Isabel with assurances that she is young and beautiful, and that this is a good time to part, since the day would have come when she no longer desired him.

At first, Isabel is shaken and furious at being dumped. Without Edgar she pictures her entire French world disintegrating. As in all Pygmalion stories, the mentor is the necessary key to the heroine's transformation. As Edgar predicted, Isabel starts to see her hero in a new light—as vain and narcissistic. Ultimately, she feels gratitude toward Edgar because he had thought her worthy of all that instruction, and that had made all the difference in how she felt about herself.

In fact, the affair has visibly transformed Isabel. Even if Edgar has repeated this affair a hundred times before, and despite her momentary vision of losing everything she gained once he ended the affair, she realizes the changes are within her and are hers to keep. Even her parents notice she is different. She knows she is now attractive to other men who are the equals or superior to her mentor. In *My Fair Lady*, Eliza Doolittle has the same realization after she attracts the interest of the prince at the ball. Henry Higgins might have created her, but she no longer needs him to pull the strings.

In *Le Divorce*, Edgar's justifications for ending the affair with Isabel were clearly self-serving, but perhaps there was also wisdom in his arguments. Some Pygmalion love stories have inevitable limitations, and even if they don't last forever, they can bring great happiness if the participants are wise enough to know when to stop.

If both members are free and can evolve into equal partners, this is a relationship that may be lasting and happy for them. But sometimes the love of a mentor should be a transitional love, a step away from a parent/child bond and a move toward independent, self-confident relationships with peers. Although this love may not last forever, it still may be gratifying to both members of the couple.

In the movie *Educating Rita*, a young working-class woman is tutored by an alcoholic English professor (played by Michael Caine) as a part of a university outreach program. The student is transformed by the professor's genuine interest in her ideas, because she regards him with awe. Gradually, she gains self-confidence and makes new friends, and worlds open up to her. But the professor has become possessive of his creation and is bitter when she prefers the company of her peers. Eventually, he is forced to accept her independence when she chooses a new educational opportunity over staying around to play nursemaid to him. He packs up and leaves for Australia, in hopes of recovering from alcoholism in a new environment, perhaps inspired by the changes he has seen in her. This was not a relationship that would last forever, but each of the partners grew in the process.

On the other hand, some women don't bounce back as quickly as Isabel Walker. They seem to be permanently damaged when their mentor abruptly decides the relationship has run its course. But just like people who never recover from the rejection of their first loves, the protégée who never gets over the end of her love affair typically had vulnerabilities that predated this relationship. If she is permanently crushed when her mentor abandons her it's usually because of earlier damage inflicted by her parents.

We all repeat love scenarios based on early experiences, in hopes of making them come out better. But when our enactments are very extreme, or too often repeated, we should see the warning sign. This usually means that we won't choose the right partner within our scenario—the one who can help us resolve our problem. Instead, we are choosing someone mainly because he allows us to relive our original trauma, a partner who is likely to confirm our worst fears instead of allowing us to rewrite the ending.

A recent true Pygmalion story that attracted much attention was reported in Joyce Maynard's memoir of her youthful affair with J. D. Salinger, who earned early fame with his novels *The Catcher in the Rye* and *Franny and Zooey*. For over thirty years, Salinger has vehemently hidden from the public and lived in a cabin in New Hampshire. For decades, he has refused to give any interviews, or to publish a single word. His work has attracted a cultlike devotion from generations of readers. So his total withdrawal from public life has long aroused interest in whether he would ever be heard from again. It was a shock, then, when Joyce Maynard wrote an intimate memoir of her affair with this man who has dedicated his life to preserving his privacy.

In 1972, when Maynard was a freshman at Yale, she enjoyed her own precocious year of fame when her essay "An Eighteen-Year-Old Looks Back on Life" was published as the lead story in the *New York Times Magazine*. Her picture appeared on the cover of the issue. Among the many letters she received was one from J. D. Salinger. She'd heard of him, although she had never read his work, and was thrilled to get a fan letter from a famous author. For a few months they corresponded, and then she dropped out of college to move into Salinger's cabin, where she lived with him for almost a year. At the time, he was fifty-three and she was eighteen.

The following spring he threw her out, and Maynard claims that for the next twenty years she still worshipped a man who would have nothing to do with her. During the year she lived with him, she adopted his eccentric beliefs and practices—her story reads like a narrative of a Svengali and his captive. But her memoir also makes it obvious that her problems and vulnerability predated her time with J. D. Salinger. Like many young women who fall in love with a parental substitute, Maynard describes parents who ignored their child's needs. A child raised this way is often the one who seeks to find a lover who will be a parent surrogate. But as in other love stories, the intensity of her need often leads her to a partner who will only reinforce the original trauma instead of helping her to grow. In Maynard's case, what started out as a Pygmalion love story evolved into a story of obsessive love after she was rejected.

Many critics attacked Joyce Maynard for betraying an intimacy from twenty-five years earlier, and robbing Salinger of the privacy that meant more to him than anything else. She knew she would be criticized, but she justified the memoir on the grounds that it was her story just as much as it was his. If Maynard robbed him of his privacy, she felt he had robbed her of her youth and destroyed her life for decades to come. But Maynard is also observant enough to trace her vulnerability back to her childhood.

Pygmalion love stories also remind us that learning is often eroticized. In *Le Divorce,* Diane Johnson's story of Isabel and her affair with Edgar is a vivid example. For women, especially, there's an intensity and excitement to what she is learning from her mentor. The pleasure in those interests can last long after the man is gone. This is true even for crushes that aren't fully realized.

Fifteen years ago, when Anna Carroll was in her late twenties and a new assistant professor of public health, she was invited to give a paper at a prestigious international conference being held in Paris—a conference held for a small group of invited scholars. She was thrilled to be included—this was a paid trip to Paris, and she was the only young woman in a group of distinguished men. There would be simultaneous translations of the papers (someone would be translating her words into French!), and her paper would be published in an international scholarly collection.

Just before the presentations began, Anna stopped in the rest room, and was shocked to find a very attractive man washing his hands. As a tourist in France, she had never used a mixed-gender bathroom. She'd grown up in a small southern town among conservative and religious African Americans. Standing beside an attractive male stranger in a French public bathroom was certainly a culture shock.

When Anna found her place on the speaker's dais, it was next to the man from the bathroom. He was an Italian physician and the editor in chief of an important European medical journal. She guessed he was in his forties, not quite old enough to be her father.

Anna's paper was enthusiastically received. Immediately after, the handsome Italian physician told her how interested he was in her ideas. Would she consider submitting a version of her paper to his journal? He was sure it would be of great interest. She agreed, of course.

He wanted to know how long she planned to stay in Paris. Anna had originally intended to return immediately after the conference, but she replied she wasn't sure. Would she be free to have dinner with him the following night? She decided on the spot to change her ticket. He asked her where she was staying. It was in the dreary hotel where the conference participants had all been put up—in a tiny room, with an uncomfortable single bed. He knew Paris well and recommended that Anna move to a more pleasant location, and gave her the name and address of a place that he thought she would find more charming.

She was in luck. The hotel he suggested had a room that was free. Her room had a grand antique bed and was decorated with a full suit of medieval armor. The large casement windows overlooked a beautiful garden that was in full June bloom.

As arranged, they met at a restaurant beside the Seine as the sun was setting. It was a perfect evening, warm with a nice breeze. The Italian physician spoke several languages, and in perfect French he inquired at the restaurant if they wouldn't mind setting up a small table outside. The waiter was happy to comply. They had dinner by candlelight, overlooking the Seine. Unlike Isabel Walker, Anna did not take notes on what he ordered for them. She was much too excited to taste the food.

At dinner, she also needed to disguise the fact that she had no memory at all of the paper the Italian doctor had delivered, right after her own presentation—not even the topic. Her heart had been pounding after her paper was greeted by applause. And Anna had been far too interested in what the physician thought of her than in anything else he had to say.

After dinner, he told her a French ballet company was giving an outdoor performance. Would she be interested in going? Although Anna liked classical music, she'd never been to a ballet. That was partly because of her family's poverty, and partly because she'd always thought of ballet as a white person's thing. The ballet was *Swan Lake*—and Anna was totally enchanted. It was a beautiful summer Paris night, the sky was filled with stars, the dancers were magical, and she was sitting beside the most sophisticated man she'd ever met. He admired her work and was anxious to present it to a large European medical audience.

They walked back to her hotel, and he took her hands and kissed Anna on both cheeks and said good night. That was certainly a letdown and anticlimax. But for all we know, the man was probably a decent and faithful husband. At the time, Anna could only fear that he'd decided she wasn't attractive or worry that she had sent the wrong cues.

When she returned to Boston, she sent him the paper, and he was as good as his word. Her article was quickly and prominently published as the lead story in the medical journal—which was a big help when she came up for tenure review. That was the end of her Paris adventure. She never again spoke to the Italian physician, but to Anna, it was still a wonderful memory.

For many years, she also became a fan of ballet—something she never would have considered before. Every time she saw *Swan Lake*, she remembered the excitement of her introduction to the dance and of her triumphant youthful visit to Paris.

Connections between intellectual or artistic excitement and romance are very common. Many women with creative or scholarly careers were first inspired by a romantic crush. They were motivated to become outstanding students because they wanted to win a teacher's attention and approval. Then, with the mentor's encouragement, a whole new world opened up—and it also gave meaning and direction for the woman's aspirations. Broadening horizons, intellectual or artistic excitement, and sexual attraction and love can't easily be separated.

The Pygmalion love story can be wonderful even if it's temporary or not fully realized. And if it does become a lasting love relationship, it must usually evolve from a parent-child model to a relation of equals. The primary obstacle is the competition for attention, the protégée's wish for independence, the mentor's reluctance to see her grow up and become her own person. But whether it's a lifelong love or a time-limited affair, it is usually one of the most exciting and pleasurable loves for both the partners.

Kate Jeffries was a rising young scholar in her biology department at a prestigious college campus. Skip Cartwright was the international star in that department and campus; he was one of the world's leading scientists in his field. Kate was twenty-nine and Skip was fifty-two. Intimate relationships between senior and junior faculty members within a department were practically forbidden on their campus, but Kate and Skip fell in love and made no effort to hide their relationship. They didn't feel like sneaking around, and Cartwright knew he would never be fired.

But this Pygmalion relationship provoked a lot of gossip and resentment. The other untenured assistant professors believed Kate had an unfair edge over them and that Cartwright would make sure she got promoted (which might reduce their chances). They also resented the fact that Kate was already socializing with the elite in their field, by virtue of being Skip's partner. That meant she had greater access to research grants and other professional rewards.

Kate had been a rising star in molecular biology before she ever met Skip. That's how she got her job in the first place. Naturally, Skip's success attracted her. Kate was ambitious, and having Skip fall in love with her made her the royal princess of their scientific discipline. Among friends, she would never deny she loved winning the crown. Yes, it was a small world they reigned over, but it was an important world and the one they lived in. Skip's stature had surely added to his attraction, as youth and beauty added to hers. But they also respected each other and had a lot in common. They had a wonderful time together and shared a passion for their work. From the start, they were forming an equal relationship despite the differences in their age and professional standing. It helped that Skip was at the peak of his career and could stay there a long time. He didn't need to worry about becoming Kate's coach or that Kate would move up the ladder to a bigger mentor. He felt secure in his place at the top.

But the gossip and resentment began to wear on the couple. Some of Skip's colleagues, very old friends, refused to have dinner with Kate. They thought Skip had created an unpleasant atmosphere in their department, which they had to live with. Hearing the complaints from other junior faculty took up a lot of their time. Some of them didn't want to socialize with Kate because the other junior faculty felt this gave her an unfair advantage over them.

Finally, Skip got so annoyed he put out the word that he'd be willing to move to any university in the country with a strong department in his field, if they would make an acceptable offer. An acceptable offer included more than the right salary and research support. It also included a tenured position for Kate, so she could come in at a senior rank too.

Almost every department would have liked to have Skip. He would put them at the top of the rankings, drawing huge grants and the best graduate students. For that matter, many would have liked to have Kate, but they didn't want to hear the accusation of nepotism or look like they were giving a twenty-nine-year-old beauty her tenure prematurely. Eventually, the couple did get their two senior positions in an outstanding campus. It created a little stink, but by the time they joined their new department, Kate was treated and viewed as one of the seniors.

Their story illustrates what can make a Pygmalion union mutually happy: the desire of both partners to move toward equality, and strong self-confidence in each. Kate could see how much Skip had given up for her: negotiating a new position and creating a new laboratory cost him precious time. Skip appreciated how Kate never made him feel old and that her admiration for him never diminished. Neither of them worried about what other people thought about them. They were very happy together and decided that the friends who couldn't accept them were not worth having as friends.

This couple's story also illustrates some of the obstacles appearing in long-term Pygmalion scenarios. Colleagues, friends, and work institutions don't always appreciate the match. People who are happy will always inspire jealousy, but it's also true that relationships like this generate real or imagined inequalities in work settings. Given that fact, Skip and Kate were wise to move to a new campus where they'd start out more like equals, not lovers who had crossed a forbidden line. Yes, it was Skip's power that got Kate her position (a little early), but when is life totally fair? Kate didn't get anything she wasn't worthy of. She had always been outstanding in her own right. If anything, she suffered a while from the innuendos that she only got her position because of Skip.

It would have been easier if they'd been able to find jobs at different institutions, and if Kate had gotten her new job independently. But academic life doesn't always offer that choice: the number of senior jobs in any geographical area is limited. There's always the option to have a commuting relationship, but that's hardly ideal. In another occupation, Kate and Skip might have found good positions in separate workplaces. Given their situation, they did the best they could.

Very soon, people forgot how Kate got her job because she was so good at her work. As they got a little older, and Kate dressed more conservatively, it became less obvious that Skip was old enough to be her father. After a few years, they were just another (successful) couple, and they always remained a happy one.

SELF-REFLECTIONS

1. If you are involved in a Pygmalion relationship, is it gratifying to both you and your partner?

2. If you are the protégée, does your partner appreciate you for who you are and what you bring to the relationship, apart from what he taught you? Or does he feel all your accomplishments are owing to him?

3. Are you in love with your partner for who he is, or just with what you can learn from him?

❤

CHAPTER THREE

Obsessive Love

I'm not going to be ignored, Dan.

—GLENN CLOSE as ALEX FORREST in *Fatal Attraction*

Haunt me . . . drive me mad! only do *not leave me in this abyss,
where I cannot find you!*

HEATHCLIFF TO CATHERINE in *Wuthering Heights by Emily Brontë*

We've all read about men who stalk and kill wives or lovers who have left them. Movies like *Fatal Attraction* or *Play Misty for Me,* the earlier Clint Eastwood movie with a similar plot, have shown us where obsessive love can lead. But you don't have to be a psychotic killer or be stalked by a rejected suitor to be severely damaged by obsessive love. Many people are tormented by this love scenario, especially in their youth. The basic plot of obsessive love is fairly well known, but it's usually misunderstood. The obsessive lover's problem isn't really that they love too intensely, but that they are trying to disguise and escape from their rage about being rejected and feeling abandoned.

Among people who suffer from obsessive love, men are more likely to vent their anger against their rejecters, while women tend to blame themselves and get depresssed. It is estimated that well over half of all the women who are murdered in this country are killed by partners they left or tried to leave. In contrast, only around 4 percent of male homicide victims are murdered by current or former intimate partners.

When women become obsessive lovers, they have the same underlying feelings as men who stalk—a deep terror and anger over abandonment, or a need to control the person they love. But in most cases women direct their rage at themselves. Deeply depressed or consumed by obsessive thoughts, these women withdraw from the real world and its opportunities for pleasure. Obsessive lovers live in the past or in a fantasy of reunion with the lost one, or a fantasy of a relationship that never really existed in the first place.

The Obsessive Love Scenario

This love scenario unfolds in a predictable way: a woman falls in love and becomes obsessed with a man. To her, he is irreplaceable. She must have this man because she feels that being attached to him will give her everything she has longed for. But no matter what he feels initially, he rejects her in the end. Sometimes her efforts to control him or her anxious and clinging demands drive him away. But more often she picks someone who never could have loved her, for reasons of his own. Either way, he pulls back or tries to end the relationship.

Even if a woman has been mistrustful and suspicious before the breakup, she will refuse to acknowledge his withdrawal or that the relationship is over. Believing that her survival depends on the relationship, she moves from feeling rejected into a mode of denial; she refuses to see that her partner doesn't love her, and she convinces herself that she will win back his love. He had become the sole focus of her existence even before he'd rejected her, and she's let everything else in her life drop away. She keeps pursuing him, trying to do things for him and make herself needed, trying to keep him from leaving.

She lives only for the relationship, even though she's increasingly having trouble repressing or disguising her rage.

But the more desperate she gets, the more he pushes her away
until a final rejection finally ends her denial of his disinterest. Now
she is filled with a rage that terrifies her. Some of that fury might
show up in mild forms of revenge, ranging from publicizing his mis-
deeds, to embarrassing and trying to make him feel guilty. But usually
the woman (and sometimes men) turns most of her anger inward.
His rejection makes her feel totally worthless, and makes her feel she
deserved the punishment she got. She seldom attacks him—instead
she attacks herself, becoming depressed or self-destructive. She may
try to kill herself, not only because of her pain but also to show the
world that he is her murderer.

The Origins of Obsessive Love

Many people assume wrongly that a woman who displays a pattern of
obsessive love is unconsciously repeating a childhood with a rejecting
father—after all, she usually seeks out men who hurt her. But this
behavior originates from a much more global sense of abandonment
in early life—and it usually involves her mother even more than her
father (since mothers are usually the primary caregivers). For whatever reason, she felt abandoned by her mother—perhaps her mother
was more involved with another child, or was sick or died when she
was young. No one else provided enough love. As a child, she was
terrified of being abandoned, and whenever she sought reassurance
from her parents, they ignored her pleas and shut her out even more.

Another early experience that can lead to obsessive love relationships is having a parent who was excessively controlling. I'm always
shocked when people tell me that when they were children or even
adolescents their mothers forced them to have regular enemas—
sometimes once or twice a week. Being subjected to that degree of
control makes a person feel passive and completely at the mercy of

the parent. It may also fill a child with rage. Later on, when that child grows up, he or she may relive this struggle over control in their relationships, but they'll want to be the one in the parental position, trying to control their partner.

The obsessive lover was filled with rage as a child, but she had no way of expressing it because she needed her parents and their love. Unconsciously, she feared her rage would destroy them—so she learned to repress it. Many of us are uncomfortable with anger (our own and the anger of others), but women with this kind of childhood are terrified of expressing their anger against people they love. The force of their anger or their early experiences of abandonment make them terrified they'll destroy or lose the person they desperately love.

Unfortunately, a woman who experienced rejection or abandonment in her childhood is always more vulnerable to feeling rejected or abandoned later in life. She often chooses situations or behaves in a way that causes her to relive her original scenario. Once she falls in love, her antennae begin searching for signs of rejection or waning affection. Any minor slight or withdrawal from the man she loves triggers intense anxiety or jealousy. She hurls accusations at him, then apologizes profusely. This wasn't what she wanted. Her motive in falling in love was to escape her pain—unconsciously, she was re-creating an old scenario because she wanted it to turn out differently.

The child who was excessively controlled will run into the same problem later when she repeats her story. If she had to submit to her parents' control, she'll try to reverse the positions and control her lover. But most often she'll choose someone who's not controllable. This will fill her with new rage and bring back the anger she felt as a child. Sometimes, the desire to control and the fear of abandonment become joined: she tries to control her lover to keep him from abandoning her. But usually her efforts will fail.

The connections among rage, controlling behavior, and fear of abandonment are obvious in the behavior of men who turn their wives or girlfriends into prisoners—cutting them off from other relationships, subjecting them to constant surveillance, ensuring their dependence. The connections may not be so obvious in female romantic obsessives. Rather than force, they try to make themselves needed or use guilt in order to keep the man from leaving.

Obsessive love is experienced in different degrees. Even relatively healthy people experience obsession at different points in their life. But not all romantic obsessives display extreme or frightening behavior: some of them control their behavior but suffer a lot in private.

For example, Patty Sherman was happily in love with Scott, a fellow intern in her medical training program. But after several months, Scott broke off the relationship and became involved with someone else in the program. Now Patty had to get along with Scott (and her rival) every day at work, even though she felt totally humiliated and abandoned. Occasionally, Scott still flirted with her, which made Patty think that one day they would get back together. Like many people in love, she believed that Scott must have the same feelings for her. She couldn't get him out of her mind, and even if she tried, she still had to see him. In fact, he often said intimate or flirtatious things to her, throwing enough encouragement her way to keep her hopes alive.

Patty may not have been reliving a total abandonment in her childhood but rather a situation in which her parents were intermittent or inconsistent in their care and attention. At times, one or both of her parents had been empathetic and caring, but then they would withdraw. Her formative trauma was that she'd had a taste of being loved and then she had lost it—her parents' love would come and go.

So when she had the boyfriend who loved her and then stopped loving her, she may have thought or fantasized that his love would start up again. That was her original trauma, and now she was trying to bring it to a happier conclusion.

On the other hand, Scott was playing out his own romantic story, which involved his own low self-esteem and avoidance of commitment. His flirting with Patty didn't mean he wanted to get back together. Instead he needed constant proof that he could defrost a woman and make her love him again even if she had seen his faults.

Many people are mildly obsessive about a love at some point in their lives. It only gets serious and frightening when the person becomes so out of touch with reality that they are willing to do anything to have the beloved, no matter how unrealistic that love is, or how much pain it brings to themselves or others.

For example, in the movie *Damage* directed by Louis Malle, a married man (played by Jeremy Irons) becomes so obsessively involved with his own son's fiancée, he pursues her without regard for the consequences. The affair destroys many lives, and the man never recovers from losing this woman. Many years later, he sees her by chance in an airport, looking like any other woman. It's her ordinariness that strikes him most deeply. He finally recognizes that his obsessive love for her was based on an image of her that he created in his own imagination.

While many of us experience obsession briefly in our lives, some make a career of it—often an escalating career. This chapter is about these true romantic obsessive lovers. Unconsciously, for the obsessively loving woman, each relationship is a reenactment of her childhood rejection and abandonment. Observers may think she enjoys her misery, but she really doesn't want to suffer. Instead, she is driven by a need to cleanse herself of rage. She desperately wants to be loved, and she chooses someone she idealizes because only someone she views as special could make up for all the pain in her past. That's why she's desperate to have him and why she feels her life depends on having this man and no other: unconsciously she's reliving an old scenario, and children don't have a choice of parents. She wants him to make up for her childhood abandonment. Instead, he rejects her as well and confirms the old pain as well as inflicting it anew.

Because her entire emotional world revolves around rejection and loss, she either picks lovers who will reject her, or she overreacts every time they want to place limits on the relationship. Usually her first love ends in rejection, and she's launched on her romantic career—escalating the drama over time, either in one relationship or a series.

Initially, when her lover doesn't come through as she wished, she can't believe he has stopped loving her (any more than a child can find another parent), so she ignores the warning signs and denies the implications of his behavior. She represses her anger and blames herself. She wants to believe that if she just tries hard enough and is forgiving enough, she can make him love her again. So she finds every reason to rationalize his withdrawal or mistreatment of her, and clings even more.

Terrified of losing his love, she throws herself into activities she can't control—calling him constantly, sending him little presents, checking up on his whereabouts, showing up at his office. She starts doing more and more for him, hoping to make herself indispensable, or to win back his love. Filling her time and her thoughts with these activities serves an even more important purpose. All this activity distracts her from her pain and her anger. As long as she keeps busy with her frantic efforts to win his love, she doesn't have to face the full force of her rage. But her needy attachment usually frightens him off.

When she finally must acknowledge his rejection, her feelings erupt, and she feels that her life is destroyed. Women are often socialized to blame themselves for the failure of a relationship. A woman who is prone to obsessive attachments will have a great deal of rage, but when the breakup occurs she has trouble venting against the person who hurt her. She's more likely to punish him with guilt—by displaying her own deterioration and threatening to kill herself. There are some women who do get revenge by embarrassing the man or exposing the affair if he is married. But even the murderous lovers in *Fatal Attraction* and *Play Misty for Me* or the exceptional women who kill the men who reject them (like Jean Harris, who killed the Scarsdale diet doctor) try to kill themselves before they end up killing their lovers. The anger that is turned against themselves is meant for their lovers, though it often hits both targets.

When men are rejected, they may find it easier to turn their lifetime's accumulated rage fully against the woman because they've been raised to equate masculinity (and their sense of identity) with acting that way. In Emily Brontë's great novel of obsessive love, *Wuthering Heights,* the hero, Heathcliff, was an orphan—abandoned by his parents. He is taken into a new home by a kind man—though he is treated like a servant rather than an adopted child. In childhood Heathcliff bonds with Cathy, the daughter of the man who rescued him, and they declare themselves twins, inseparable for life. But when Cathy grows up, she distances herself from Heathcliff and marries a more socially cultivated boy who lives nearby. The rejection is totally devastating to Heathcliff because Cathy's love had always been the primary consolation in his painful, orphaned existence. After Cathy betrays him, his life is reduced to anger and revenge, until he destroys everything he loves. Then he kills himself in order to be with the lover that he lost.

The anxiety of not having a solid identity and the need to shore it up is also another reason people experience obsessive love. This vulnerability exists on a continuum. Everyone who is in love feels that their self-esteem depends on their beloved, because they have merged their identity with that person to some degree. But most people don't lose their whole identity in love or fall completely apart when they experience romantic rejection. They usually get over it and find someone new. The difference has to do with whether the lover has a sense of his or her own independent identity and its boundaries. Some people identify with their love object so profoundly that it overrides their own individuality. When this occurs, romantic rejection is devastating, as it was for Heathcliff.

Even young people who were well cared for by their parents can experience a phase of obsessive love because their identities are undeveloped. Like people who have more extreme and lifelong problems with obsessive love, young lovers often feel the need to merge with love objects they idealize. Their boundaries are more fluid, and when they fall in love, they totally identify with their love object. Like older romantic obsessives, they can get really hurt because for them so much is riding on a particular relationship. As we grow older (or work out our problems with romantic obsession) our sense of ourselves becomes more firmly demarcated. Only adults with severe self-esteem problems feel the need to merge with someone else.

But some people never develop that sense of boundaries in adulthood, while others lose the identity that sustained them in their youth. They idealize a lover and come to believe that this person has strengths they need; their deep identification with that person makes them feel completed. When people like this are rejected by their love objects, they feel terrified, like abandoned children, because they feel cut off from the source of everything they needed. These are the people who often wind up becoming stalkers or who fall into a serious depression when they lose a lover.

So the problem of romantic obsession exists on a continuum. It's a phase that some of us pass through and grow out of, while for others it's a progressive illness that strips away any real life or possibility of happiness. By looking at the range of cases, we can also learn something about how people overcome this problem.

Liz Tropper's life offers one illustration of a love-obsessed career. In college and afterward she was very appealing to men—she was warm, funny, brilliant, and beautiful. She was a bit too intense for some men, but many found her attractive. During her sophomore year at UCLA, she met her first love—a graduate student named Doug. Liz adored him and came to feel that she couldn't live without him. He was strongly drawn to her too, but he was always unfaithful and he didn't want to get married.

Liz felt humiliated by Doug's infidelity and his refusal to commit. Over a period of years, she also had to make increasing concessions in order to retain the deteriorating relationship. Like many women who develop obsessive attachments, she was willing to bear the pain and humiliation because the alternative—giving up the relationship—was just not an option. She couldn't imagine a life without Doug. For five years they fought, broke up, and then started over again. Like many people who are obsessively attached, she refused to acknowledge the obvious—that this relationship was never going to work. Although her feelings of anger occasionally broke through, and she saw her boyfriend's flaws, Liz still idealized Doug and felt inferior and unworthy of him. If he didn't love her enough, she believed that it was because something was wrong with her, something she could fix if she only tried harder. Finally, their relationship definitively ended when Doug got a job in northern California.

Liz was devastated, but soon she met a rising young actor who asked her to be his date for several highly publicized social events. She spent weeks getting ready for each party and felt like Cinderella at the ball. Unfortunately this prince always disappeared at midnight. For months she ignored all the signs that he was gay—once again, her feeling that he was her dream come true kept her from seeing what should have been obvious. The actor never lied, misled, or meant to hurt her—but Liz couldn't see that she was just his "date" for formal events. He also needed to protect his career (this was in the 1980s and it's probably still true), so he couldn't spell it out for her explicitly. Liz, though otherwise bright and perceptive, believed for months that eventually they would become a couple.

It was the next affair that really did her in: a five-year descent into degradation and self-hatred. Liz met Phil when she was twenty-six and beginning to succeed as an entertainment lawyer. Phil was unhappily married and the father of two young boys. He'd been having affairs throughout his marriage, but he left his wife, Shelly, only after getting involved with Liz. Shelly became so depressed she started drinking too much and became addicted to tranquilizers.

At first, Liz mainly felt contempt for Shelly. (In fact, most of us find it hard to empathize with romantic obsessives, because we don't like to recognize those desperate and dependent tendencies in ourselves.) But over the years of her relationship with Phil, Liz found herself sinking into unprecedented humiliation, abuse, and dependence. She began to see herself as a helpless victim who didn't have the strength to save herself.

She knew Phil was sleeping around, probably with prostitutes, but that didn't end her attachment to him. After five years he broke up with Liz and started to date other women. Liz was so desperate on her birthday that she went to his house, uninvited. He wasn't alone, and he threw her out. She felt humiliated and desexualized, but she missed him so much that she felt she didn't exist anymore.

Not long after, Phil lost his job, and Liz loaned him large sums of money, though she knew he would never pay her back. He had never had the charm or the talent of her earlier loves, and her friends couldn't imagine what Liz saw in him. She seemed to be suffering and degrading herself more for a man who was even worse than her previous boyfriends. Ironically, as Liz was deteriorating, Phil's former wife, Shelly, was growing stronger. She went to AA, stopped drinking and taking tranquilizers, returned to school, got an advanced degree and a good job, and made a happy second marriage—this time to a man who allowed her to be the dominant partner.

For a few years after Phil left her, Liz had no serious relationships. She dated and had lots of male friends, and had a successful career, but she avoided any romantic relationships. Then one of her closest friends died in a drowning accident while vacationing in Mexico. This was a terrible shock to Liz, and she started to realize that life doesn't go on forever.

One of her friends insisted on fixing Liz up with a really nice man—he was totally unlike any of her former lovers. David adored her and thought she was the best company and the most terrific human being on earth. For David, it was love at first sight—a match made in heaven. They shared the same interests and hobbies and had similar backgrounds. From the start, he had no doubt he wanted to spend the rest of his life with her.

At first, Liz felt this was just not going to work. She wasn't used to a man who was honest and straightforward and who adored her— a man who did not present any obstacles. It made her extremely uncomfortable. She was not used to this scenario, and now she had to face her own conflicts and fears about commitment because David was clear about his love. But Liz is a very intelligent woman who had come to recognize her destructive patterns, even if she didn't fully understand where they came from.

Gradually she came to love David deeply, and when Liz was thirty-six and David thirty-one, they married. Eight years have passed, and they are still very happy and rarely have a fight. In the end, it was not an obsessive kind of love that erased all of Liz's anger and pain. It was the love of a really good man whom she was finally able to appreciate, once she was ready to give up the unhappy romantic scenario she had lived out for fifteen years.

What allowed Liz (and Phil's first wife, Shelly) to give up a love story that made them miserable? First of all, both women ultimately developed their own strengths and interests and had rich lives of their own. They did not allow their romantic obsessions to rob their lives of any other meaning. It's hard to escape from the grip of an obsession and to feel that you have your own identity when there isn't much else going on in your life. The death of Liz's friend also made her face her own mortality—the fact that she wasn't that young anymore and wouldn't live forever. People who tend to live in a fantasy world often don't see that time is passing. It takes something dramatic to make them see they have lost years living an imaginary life.

Equally important, both Liz and Shelly consciously picked different kinds of men to marry after leaving behind their obsessive romantic scenarios—men who were in love with them and who never made them feel abandoned. These men allowed them to feel more in control of the relationship.

Most love stories can have a happy or unhappy outcome, depending on one's choices and behavior. But obsessive love relationships are the most difficult to resolve—they rarely work out well. The motives behind them are too problematic, and obsessive lovers usually need to change their behavior before they can have a happy relationship. Liz succeeded because, first of all, she always had the potential for being an independent person. She had a rich life and worked at something she liked. She also had many friends who adored her. But she was able to change her love scenario only after she recognized her pattern and consciously chose a man who was very different from those who attracted her in the past.

Also, for once, she chose a man she didn't need to pursue. He was the one who had to win her. This is the shift that must occur in someone prone to obsessive attachments. There must be a change in the balance of involvement, and women like Liz must learn to love men who need them and want them.

Because David had no conflicts about loving her, he didn't do things that stirred up Liz's sensitivity to rejection and abandonment. In time, he made her feel safe, and she no longer responded to every slight or withdrawal as if they were the prelude to a global rejection.

Is Masochism an Element in Love Obsessions?

Many people say that women who can't give up unrequited love must surely be masochists—and they get themselves into painful or degrading attachments because they are looking for punishment. But this is not at all true for the vast majority of women drawn into obsessive relationships. In fact, the reverse is true—they fall in love in order to erase their pain.

In her classic essay "The Woman in Love" from *The Second Sex*, Simone de Beauvoir explains why love may become masochistic, even though the original motive was not to suffer. De Beauvoir observed that the woman who loses herself in a man wants to avoid seeing herself in a powerless, humiliating position. She wants to merge with a man to elevate herself—but ironically, that choice takes her into an emotional hell.

According to de Beauvoir, she sees her lover as a god and wants to share in his glory. She tries to make herself indispensable to him. As long as the man accepts her sacrifices, de Beauvoir observed, the woman feels no self-hatred. But from her vulnerable position, it is easy for her to fall into masochism: it can happen if he loves her less than she wants, or even if he's innocently interested in something unrelated to her. For he is the whole world to her, and any lesser involvement on his part feels like abandonment to her. Sometimes she feels abandoned when he merely falls asleep. It is the loss of herself that makes her so vulnerable to self-hatred, but her original motive for falling in love was not to suffer but rather to raise her self-esteem.

Letting Go of Obsessions

Obsessive love is in some ways like an addiction, and to overcome it, one can learn from those who overcome addictions. The first thing you have to do is stay away from temptation. If you are an alcoholic who wants to stop drinking, you know you can't keep alcohol in the house or meet your friends in a bar. If you are trying to lose weight and are addicted to desserts, you don't bring a chocolate cake home and expect it to last for a week.

In the same way, obsessive lovers have a lot of emotions and beliefs that need to be worked on, but it's always easier to change the simple behaviors first. That means putting the brakes on behaviors that are expressions of your obsessions—behaviors that you know are going to make you miserable. It means you don't drop in, unannounced, at your ex-boyfriend's house because it's your birthday and you're lonely and miserable. He knew (or should have known) it was your birthday. If he had wanted to be with you, he would have. When you want to call someone who has rejected you or drive by his house late at night to see whether he's with someone else, you must stop yourself. Don't send him little gifts or write him any letters. If he calls you in order to stay on friendly terms, don't return the call. You can't be friends with him now. It will only stimulate your fantasies.

Once you recognize that your constant thoughts about your lover are crowding out any chance of real happiness, you must label these thoughts as self-destructive. Love obsessions lead to an empty life. To recover from them, one has to build up a real life and do everything possible to keep obsessional thoughts under control. That means meeting new people and doing interesting things.

This is hard when all you want to think about is your obsession. So if you are living your life in a romantic obsession you need to modify your behavior. Whenever thoughts of your lover pop into your head, divert yourself by doing something requiring total mental concentration. This will keep you from having obsessive thoughts. If you're not yet ready to part with your obsessions completely, limit the time you allow yourself to have them—confine it to a few minutes a day. When a child's temper tantrum won't end, some parents tell their child to yell and scream all he or she wants for five or ten minutes, but then he or she must stop. Tell your destructive obsessions they can have ten minutes a day to express themselves, but once the time is up they'll have to go on hold until tomorrow.

At first, you'll avoid the small choices that will make you miserable. Eventually, you'll avoid the big mistakes that can ruin your life. Like Liz, you'll run from the men who used to attract you and you'll pick a man who wants to be with you.

The people who have the most extreme obsessive attachments typically repeat this scenario. But some people also play out this love story just once. They fall into this unaccustomed role because they meet someone who evokes an old memory from childhood—usually involving an unresolved issue with a parent.

Randy Ryan is a good example of a one-time obsessional lover. She departed from her usual pattern of being the one in control of a relationship and fell in love with a man who was far more controlling than she. Randy was used to having the upper hand, but this lover never let her have it. She submitted to a lot of humiliation because he was playing the parental role in reliving her original struggle over control.

Randy had always been the dominant partner. In her first marriage and earlier affairs, she had all the power and control. She was the one who loved less and who always wanted more time and room for herself. However, she'd always felt unsatisfied by these relationships because she wanted a man who was her equal—someone others admired as well.

She started her one and only obsessive love affair when she was twenty-nine. She was a young, ambitious marine biologist and was unusually successful for her age. At a scientific conference, she met and became attracted to a colleague, Rupert Donnelly, who was somewhat older and highly respected in their field. Her first marriage had been over for only a year, so she wasn't really looking for a permanent partner. But Rupert was an independent man—one who couldn't be owned, and she was attracted by the challenge. When she asked mutual acquaintances about him, they told her he was married and a family man—all work and no play—and they assured Randy that he was not available. This did not deter her.

The next time she attended a conference where he'd be (and where she was presenting a paper herself), she arranged for a friend to drop her off. That way she could ask Rupert for a lift home. Randy was accustomed to taking charge and going after what she wanted. "I asked him to hold my purse before I walked onstage, to make sure he'd still be there when I got off."

Her plan worked. They left the conference together and Rupert drove Randy home. She invited him in and told him about her marriage ending. Rupert told her that he was in an unhappy marriage— and that his wife was an alcoholic. He appeared very solid and sane. He seemed like a devoted family man with a marriage that had gone wrong because he picked an alcoholic wife. He stayed for a couple of hours, and they kissed at the door. Randy told herself she wasn't breaking up anything that wasn't already ending.

Soon they were having an affair, although Rupert's availability was limited because of his work. His marriage was ending, and it upset him. Randy didn't think she was doing anything self-destructive because Rupert was a successful professional, committed to his work, and they shared so many interests. "I thought if people were stratifying us, we'd be in the same cut—he slightly above because he was older." This was important to Randy, because she'd always wanted a man who was as successful as she was.

From the start, she began accepting problems in the relationship. Rupert always arrived late for a date. If they were supposed to have three hours together, he came two hours late. By then, she'd be furious and they'd fight fof forty minutes and make up in the last twenty. "He'd come late because he was working, and he was selfish and didn't want to stop. He was late from the very first date. He ran his life for himself. Whenever we were meeting I'd get happy and all ready. Then I'd expect him to be thirty minutes late, and when an hour passed, I'd go crazy. He'd say, 'This is how I am.' I'd fight, but I put up with it, so I stopped being an equal."

Randy lost equal footing in other ways from the start. For a long time, Rupert didn't want to leave his wife and wanted to keep both relationships. After all, why should he inconvenience himself as long as Randy was willing to accept the arrangement? Several months into the affair he even said to her: "Why should I leave her when I can have you both?"

Randy, who had always been in control, soon found that Rupert was going to control their sexual relationship as well. "Once, we were making love, and I said 'lower' or 'harder,' and he said, 'No, I'll make love in my own way.' I lost my sexual feeling. I was shocked. He was telling me I wasn't going to direct the relationship."

She tried to avoid arguments when he disappointed her, because she could never win. After they'd fight, they'd break up, and she had to grovel and plead for him to come back.

Rupert, on the other hand, never apologized for any of his behavior. From the start, it was clear that he loved her less than she loved him, and that the relationship was less important to him. Six months into the affair, he finally separated from his wife, but he continued having sex with her. And she wasn't Randy's only rival.

A year and a half into the relationship, after he'd returned from a trip, they were in bed and Rupert seemed rather cool. Randy recalls what happened next. "He said, 'I have something to tell you.' I went cold. He said, 'I'm in love with someone else.' My heart dropped out. I physically flinched. I asked who she was, and it turned out it was someone he had met on a ski trip six months before. He'd been lying all that time. I didn't believe he was capable of that. It was like your mother saying I don't love you."

The other woman turned out to be a twenty-year-old fitness trainer. This really offended Randy because she valued her intellect and professional accomplishments, which, it turned out, weren't so important to Rupert after all. He told Randy he still loved her, but he also loved Susan, the other woman.

Randy lost the little control she still had. She went through Rupert's pockets and his bureau and found her rival's letters. They were written in babyish script, with poems she considered infantile. Randy read the letters and felt their author was so dumb and puerile, she would die. When she confronted Rupert and asked him how he could possibly love such a woman, he blew up.

Not wanting to face the truth, Randy decided that Rupert was running away from her rather than toward Susan, because this explanation made her feel more in control. Susan turned out to have more self-respect than she did and broke up with Rupert a few months later.

But after the affair with Susan ended, things only got worse. Rupert would no longer promise Randy monogamy. "He told me he loved me but not enough. He told me he didn't want to live with me. I think I loved him so passionately because he was unreachable and so smart, and so looked-up-to by his peers."

The affair continued on and off, in this manner, for five years. Randy was making increasing concessions to keep it alive. During these years, Randy got pregnant twice and had two abortions. For the first one, Rupert wasn't even in town. The second time, she wanted to have the baby, but Rupert said it would ruin his life. She went through with the abortion rather than alienate him, but it killed off some of her love—and a year later they broke up. Randy was now thirty-four years old and she knew it was time to find a man who wanted a family.

"My friends treated the relationship like my sickness. But I was proud to be going with him—I was proud that I was woman enough to handle him, this powerful personality."

After five years of suffering through the affair with Rupert, Randy met another man and married him six months later. Now they're expecting their first child. The man she married is much nicer than Rupert, and Randy reverted to her usual pattern—she is the dominant partner. Tim gives her the freedom to be moody and difficult. Now she is the one who wants more time to herself, and she finds herself acting like Rupert at times. "When I was with Rupert, if I wanted to discuss something, he'd see it as nagging if I tried several ways of talking about it. He'd just say, 'It's been discussed.' Now Tim is more likely to do that, and I'll say, 'I do not wish to discuss this further.' "

On the other hand, Randy is more forgiving of what she sees as Tim's faults than Rupert was with her. "I may see a few little things I don't like in Tim, but I see them as minor, whereas Rupert could never get by my faults. I may cut off a discussion with Tim, but I won't think he's not right for me because he wanted to have it."

When they first broke up, she missed how passionately she felt about Rupert, but she can see that it was never a real relationship. The man she married is more of a partner, while Rupert had always felt like more of a father figure to her. Because she was already successful in her work when she'd met Rupert, Randy had never viewed him as a mentor. But she had admired him, and being linked with him made her feel more powerful.

In retrospect, she wouldn't have had the affair with Rupert, but Randy sees that she learned some things from that experience that allowed her to have a better relationship with Tim. Never winning an argument with Rupert taught her about self-discipline. "I learned to hold my tongue, and to be less emotional. These things have helped me. If I yelled at Rupert, he was out the door, so I learned not to. That's a good thing to learn. There's no reason to yell. When I'm angry now, I stay cool. There are some things you just shouldn't say."

Randy also learned she needs control in a relationship, and stopped devaluing any man who would let her have it. Her relationship with Rupert gave her the opportunity to relive her control struggles with her parents, and to see that being controlled didn't make her happy.

Randy and Liz are very different people, and the marriages they made are different. Liz wound up in an equal relationship, Randy in one that let her have a little more control. But they both wound up with good men who loved them, the kind of man each needed.

These women also show that people who are otherwise strong and talented, people who have self-confidence in other areas of their lives, can still be vulnerable and lose their identities in romantic obsessions. Obviously Liz and Randy had a firm sense of themselves professionally, so they had a platform for regaining their independence and self-respect. But the fictional and real-life stories of people with the most extreme obsessions shed greater light on the anger and rage that is cloaked with love in these scenarios, the anger that isn't so obvious in people like Randy and Liz.

Consider some famous examples from fiction and movies. In *Fatal Attraction,* Glenn Close's love for the married Michael Douglas goes through two transformations after their one-night stand. First, she becomes self-destructive, slashing her wrists to try to bind him with guilt. When that doesn't work her rage is finally directed at him—in escalating degrees: destroying his car with acid, invading his home, kidnapping his daughter, and killing her pet rabbit. Finally, she works her way up to trying to stab him to death with a huge butcher knife.

When I first saw *Fatal Attraction,* many people in the movie theater cheered when Douglas's wife kills Glenn Close before she can stab her husband. Few people expressed any sympathy for Close's character—she had turned into a monster, and we don't like to see how capable we are of monstrous behavior.

In *Play Misty for Me,* Clint Eastwood is a late-night radio host who becomes the target of an obsessional fan. She seduces him one night, and then he has a real problem—an increasingly violent and deranged admirer who won't leave him alone. She moves through the characteristic stages of a very sick woman who's been romantically rejected: first, she refuses to accept that the Eastwood character is trying to cool out the relationship. Then she spies on him and breaks into his house.

When Eastwood's old girlfriend returns to the scene, the rejected lover's fury is turned inside out: first, she attempts suicide and finally she works up to murder. At several points in the story, she moves back and forth between apologizing, pleading, and displaying her rage. But the anger is always ready to explode from the very first time Eastwood tries to impose limits on the relationship.

Adolescent Obsessive Love

One of the most brilliant and sympathetic portraits of obsessive love is Scott Spencer's novel *Endless Love.* Spencer's hero, eighteen-year-old David Axelrod, is in love not only with Jade but also with her entire family. Compared with his own supremely selfish and insensitive mother and his passive, depressed father, the Butterfield home seems a paradise inhabited by gods. But when Jade's father decides his sixteen-year-old daughter is getting too seriously involved, he banishes David from their home for at least a month, until the end of the school year.

David can't bear the month's separation and is terrified he'll lose the girl who has filled his life with meaning. Although he intends no harm, at least consciously, he sets a fire on the porch of her home, fantasizing that when he rescues the Butterfields they'll take him back in. But the fire gets out of control, and as punishment David is sent to a mental hospital in lieu of prison.

Soon after, the Butterfields divorce—largely because of David's impact on the family. Later, when he's released from the hospital, he immediately heads for New York, looking for Jade (violating the condition of his freedom). Jade's father spots David as he's crossing a street. Furious at seeing that David is on the loose, Butterfield lunges toward him and is struck and killed by an automobile. In the end, David must spend ten years under lock and key because of his inability to separate from Jade and his refusal to give up hoping for their reunion.

Through it all, David seems the innocent victim of other people's anger. And yet one also suspects there must be repressed rage lying within—even if he suffers more than anyone else. After all, by the end of the novel, David's love has set in motion a great deal of suffering. Spencer's portrait of David's mother explains why David clings to his dream of love at any cost: he must have felt abandoned all his life. Obsessive male lovers are rarely portrayed in a way that invites identification or sympathy. Spencer's narrator is a rare and illuminating exception. Against the background of his cold, narcissistic mother, David's love for Jade seems almost pure and heroic.

In contrast, John Fowles's novel *The Collector* portrays a deranged man who captures a woman and keeps her chained in his cellar. Finally he kills her out of fear that she will escape and leave him. He would rather have her dead than risk losing his beloved prisoner. The story illustrates the ties between obsessional attachments, rage, the need to control, and the fear of abandonment.

This constellation forms the core of the domestic violence stories that wind up in the news. According to a February 15, 2000, report in the *New York Times,* in almost half the cases in which men killed their wives or girlfriends, the woman was breaking off the relationship. In many other cases, the killer said he felt abandoned because he believed his partner had been sexually unfaithful. Women are in the greatest danger right after they have left their partners: over half of these murders occur within two months of a separation, and 85 percent within a year.

Since women (and men) can't always protect themselves from lovers they are leaving, they need to look out for the danger signs and avoid partners who show characteristics of obsessional love. Young women, especially, often misinterpret their boyfriend's extreme jealousy or possessive behavior as signs of love.

Liz and Randy demonstrate that it is possible to change this unhappy romantic scenario—though usually the change comes only after suffering a great deal of pain. The key to changing the story depends on a strengthening of self-esteem and independent identity. This is as true for men as it is for women.

In the movie, *Mr. Jealousy,* the narrator (Eric Stoltz) destroys all of his romantic relationships because as soon as he falls in love he becomes extremely jealous. Instead of being in the relationships, he becomes consumed with investigating his girlfriends' fidelity.

The Stoltz character finally meets the woman of his dreams (Annabella Sciorra), and she returns his love. But again, he becomes obsessed with her former boyfriends and is certain she is secretly sleeping with them. One, in particular, preys on his mind. Stoltz, a would-be writer, has never had the self-confidence to develop his talents: the ex-boyfriend happens to be a successful novelist. He becomes so consumed by his jealous fantasies of this rival that he never has time to spend with his girlfriend.

In fact, there's some reason for Stoltz to be jealous (as there often is, in the case of obsessive lovers). His girlfriend isn't entirely faithful, but largely because his obsessive jealousy has caused her to feel neglected and alienated. At one point, he criticizes her for having sex with him on their first date. She tells him it was because she liked him so much. But he's bothered, because he thinks if she slept with him so readily, she'll have sex with anybody. "You're jealous of yourself?" she asks him incredulously.

Inevitably, they break up. This time, his pain is so deep that he knows he must change. He moves away to enter a creative writing program. This is actually a sensible decision—a step toward changing himself and laying the foundation to have a healthy relationship. Often, the only way to clear one's mind of an obsession is to concentrate one's mind on something else—preferably something more constructive.

When Obsessions Take the Place of Real Life

The most extreme obsessions can flourish in the most minimal relationship. One of the most interesting published case histories of a romantic obsession was written by the psychoanalyst Irvin D. Yalom. He named his book *Love's Executioner* because this described how he felt while treating a seventy-year-old patient who had allowed a love obsession to replace her real life. He believed that the only way to help Thelma regain any real life was to destroy her romantic illusions. But she felt that renouncing her romantic hopes was the equivalent of dying. Thelma warned him that his cure might actually kill her.

Thelma had spent most of her life in a marriage that lacked intimacy. For the past twenty years, she'd been in treatment for depression. About eleven years before seeing Yalom, at the age of sixty, she had gone into treatment with a young psychotherapist, Matthew—a man thirty years her junior. After a year and a half, Matthew had stopped treating her when he accepted a full-time job. They happened to meet a year later, and she and Matthew had a twenty-seven-day love affair. Those twenty-seven days had been the most important thing in Thelma's entire life. But Matthew had suddenly broken off the relationship and had stopped returning her phone calls after she attempted suicide over losing him. This did not stop Thelma from leaving messages on Matthew's machine, which she continued to do for eight years.

During these eight years, she told Yalom, she had spent every moment thinking of Matthew and wondering what had gone wrong. She knew she was "living her life eight years ago," but she refused to give up the hope of a reunion, even if the chances of that happening were only "one percent." In fact, she felt that she would be satisfied if she could just talk with Matthew for five minutes once a year. That would be enough to make her happy.

At first, Yalom didn't know what to make of this story. Had she imagined the whole thing? Was Matthew a sociopath who had exploited his patient for his own sexual needs? Yalom knew that therapists who do this generally choose young and attractive patients, not much older women.

Yalom was also frustrated that Thelma would not even relate to him as a therapist. She was so consumed with Matthew that Yalom didn't exist. He believed his only chance to pry his patient from her obsession was to try to make her real life a little bit richer. But her life and her marriage were so empty there was little to build on. Her illusions about Matthew and their mutual love were irrational, but Yalom wondered if he should really take away the fantasy that provided the greatest pleasure in her life.

Finally, when Yalom failed to penetrate her obsessions, he suggested a three-way meeting with Thelma, Matthew, and himself. For the first time he saw his patient perk up; she felt that Matthew would come if Yalom called. The next week, Thelma arrived at his office looking remarkably younger and smartly dressed. For the first time, she wasn't wearing a jogging outfit. She'd called Matthew herself to tell him about Dr. Yalom's proposal, and he'd immediately called back and said he would come.

The meeting was a revelation to Yalom. Matthew explained that eight years earlier he had suffered a psychotic break after pursuing a long and solitary meditation in India. He'd been hospitalized for a month and had run into Thelma on the street the day after he was released. He was still very disturbed, and he couldn't even distinguish his own self from Thelma, or her desires from his own. When she wanted to have sex with him, he complied.

After a few weeks, Matthew was having hallucinations, and was hospitalized again. When he was released, six weeks later, he learned that Thelma had tried to kill herself.

Matthew was haunted by guilt at the damage he'd inflicted, and at first he returned her calls. But when Thelma wouldn't stop calling or showing up at his office, his own therapist had advised him to break off all contact with her. He had given up his profession as a psychotherapist and had a new occupation. Many times Matthew had tried to tell Thelma what had happened, and why he couldn't be in contact with her, but for eight years, she had refused to hear. He did care what happened to her and thought about her every day. When he finished his explanation Thelma burst into tears and accused him of being insincere.

When Yalom finally saw the true story unfolding before him, he wondered why Thelma had never relayed any of this to him. Once he looked at Matthew as another patient rather than as a therapist, he saw him more as the victim than the exploiter.

After that meeting, Thelma's anger at Matthew erupted. Now, Yalom thought he could make some progress and convince Thelma that there had never really been a love affair, even a twenty-seven-day love affair, because Matthew had been psychotic at the time. But Yalom was mistaken. This pronouncement punctured her most cherished fantasy—her twenty-seven days of love. Thelma sank into a deeper depression. Not long after, Thelma announced she was discontinuing therapy.

Yalom was deeply distressed, but he could not talk Thelma out of leaving. In the end, he decided that she might have been right. He had been love's executioner, and perhaps she was correct in observing that more treatment might kill her. When he called Thelma some weeks later, she assured him that she no longer needed therapy. She had met with Matthew again, and it had done wonders for her. They had agreed to meet for a chat every once in a while.

Yalom never saw Thelma again, but six months later she kept her appointment with a research team that was evaluating the impact of therapy. The researchers concluded that of all the patients in the group, Thelma had shown the greatest improvement. They noted that the patient seemed to benefit from the therapist's strategy of bringing an estranged friend into the therapeutic process.

As Yalom explains, Thelma's case illustrates how a romantic obsession, even when it is a total illusion, can offer a substitute for real satisfaction and real relationships in an otherwise empty life. The problem with obsessions is that they don't leave room for reality. In Thelma's case, there was so little to build on that there wasn't much chance of developing new interests and relationships. But it's a different story for people who could have a real life—people who are barely twenty years old and equally lost in their romantic obsessions.

I have observed that many female college students who do not have boyfriends often develop romantic fantasies about male friends. They even become obsessive, in the sense that these fantasy relationships dominate their lives. All their time is spent thinking about their male friend, looking for signs that he is interested in more than friendship and feeling devastated and jealous when he sees other women. Some of these young women feel heartbroken and abandoned when their friend fails to act as a romantic partner would.

These women don't show the same rage as the true obsessionals

I've described—but like them, and like Thelma, they use these fantasies to fill a void that exists because they are not in a real relationship. Depressed about being uninvolved and unloved, these fantasies provide some of the romantic and sexual excitement they are missing and give a small boost to their self-esteem. But the romance exists only inside their heads. Sometimes these unrequited loves for friends go on for years and years. The danger is that these substitute fantasies enable them to avoid reciprocal relationships.

Women who develop unrequited crushes usually confide their feelings to their friends. After all, one of the purposes of this surrogate romance is to have something to talk about when your friends discuss their love lives. Invariably, their friends offer them the sensible advice to check out their fantasies—to find out, once and for all, if their feelings are returned so they will stop wasting their time on something that's not going to happen. But the thought of testing the fantasy is generally too threatening for these women—they fear they will lose their friend altogether if they express their real feelings, and they also don't want to lose their illusions.

When fantasies are short-term substitutes between relationships, they are pleasant and not very dangerous fillers. But when they replace a real life and real attachments, they turn into a love scenario of Avoidance, as we will see in chapter 7. In other cases, the fantasy becomes so real that the woman builds up to the jealousy and anger of a true obsessive.

Carol Weil has been in love with her best male friend at college since freshman year. They are close and have spent a lot of time together. But Carol has never told Peter that she has romantic feelings for him. As long as Peter didn't have a girlfriend, Carol wasn't suffering terribly. But by sophomore year, he started dating and told Carol about these girls.

She felt horribly betrayed and cried like a woman left at the altar. Whenever Peter would break up with one of his girlfriends, he'd tell Carol everything that was wrong in the relationship. This would lift her hopes and her self-esteem for a few weeks—that is, until he found someone new.

This pattern continued into Carol's senior year. All this time, she had not dated a single boy. Her friends pleaded with her to tell Peter how she felt and find out if there was any hope. But she refused, rationalizing that she might lose him altogether as a friend if he knew how she felt and he didn't feel the same way.

Things came to a head when Carol invited Peter to her family home in New Hampshire for Thanksgiving dinner. She had hinted to her family that he was more than a friend, though when they tried to extract more details she was highly secretive. When Peter didn't show up, they waited to start the dinner. Her sisters complained that the food was being ruined. It was snowing outside, and Carol had visions of Peter being killed in a car crash. Somehow that was more comforting than concluding he'd simply forgotten about her invitation. Being a smart young woman, Carol realized that her worries about his death were probably a reflection of her anger.

She wasn't able to reach Peter (there was no answer at home), so for hours, she wavered between worry and rage. Her family tried to be lighthearted, but they could see she was distraught. Carol felt totally humiliated. Her family was concerned she was being hurt by a boy who didn't care about her. Around nine o'clock, Peter called and said it looked like he wasn't going to make it. He'd gotten held up at a previous commitment, the weather was terrible, he was really sorry and hoped he could meet her family another time.

When Carol confronted Peter back at school, he told her he had a very different memory of their agreement. He recalled telling Carol that he'd like to come, but he was going to another party first. In his mind, he'd always pictured her family starting their dinner without him—he'd thought all along he would join them for dessert. Whatever the original conversation, they clearly had very different emotional investments. Peter couldn't understand why Carol was so furious with him, or what he had done that was so terrible.

This pattern of living in a relationship that doesn't exist is unfortunately common. One variation is the woman who develops an obsessive passion for a man who has no more than a casual interest—perhaps he comes around once in a while and spends the night when he's in between serious involvements. In this case, there is some basis for her romantic feelings—at first—but she refuses to recognize that her love is not returned at the same level it is given. Like the woman who lives on romantic illusions about a platonic friendship, this might start out as a compensating fantasy. It becomes more obsessive and destructive when she allows the relationship to become the center of her life.

Romantic obsessions are not restricted to loners or psychotics who live in imaginary worlds. Liz and Randy and other obsessive lovers spend far more time feeling rejected and suspicious than enjoying their real lover's company. Even relationships that begin with a mutual attraction, as theirs did, can deteriorate quickly if one of the partners is drawn to this scenario and if she's chosen a partner who's unlikely to help her resolve it.

In the popular television series *Friends*, Ross's dream of winning Rachel's love finally comes true, but it happens only after he starts to transfer his affections to a different woman. Ross had to become less involved with Rachel before she could feel attracted to him. At the start of their affair, their love is mutual, but Ross's typical pattern of feeling jealous and suspicious ultimately destroys their relationship. Even when obsessive lovers have actual partners, their obsessive thoughts and fantasies wind up consuming their lives.

The only way out of this kind of self-defeating pattern is for the obsessive lover to engage in constructive activities and real life. She needs to meet new people and do things that will raise her self-esteem. Anything that requires mental concentration tends to be most helpful. She'll be free of romantic obsessions as long as her mind is filled with something else. Taking a course that interests her, pursuing a new interest or skill, doing something demanding that has a deadline (and therefore forces her concentration so she can't slip back into obsessing)—all these things will help pry her from her obsession and help her feel better about herself.

In obsessive relationships there's usually a calamitous inequality—one partner is greatly more involved than the other. The relationship is usually doomed unless the one who loves more can shift some of her emotional energy to other interests and persons. Even if the relationship doesn't last, learning to control her obsessions will help her the next time she falls in love.

SELF-REFLECTIONS

1. Do you find yourself acting like the obsessive lovers in this chapter? Do you think about nothing else but your lover, while the rest of your life has vanished?

2. Do you feel annihilated when a partner withdraws from you or extremely anxious if he or she refuses to be controlled by you?

3. If you think you may be enacting this scenario, what are you doing about it? Are you taking constructive steps to stop your obsessive thoughts and activities? Are you trying to engage in other activities that will force you to focus on something else and make you feel better about yourself while you develop new talents and meet new people?

♥

CHAPTER FOUR

The Downstairs Woman and the Upstairs Man

Do you think, because I am poor, obscure, plain, and little, I am soulless and heartless? You think wrong!—I have as much soul as you,—and full as much heart! And if God had gifted me with some beauty, and much wealth, I should have made it as hard for you to leave me, as it is now for me to leave you.

—JANE EYRE to EDWARD ROCHESTER in *Jane Eyre* by Charlotte Brontë

The Cinderella fairy tale never seems to lose its emotional appeal, and its adult variation is the Upstairs-Downstairs love plot. This is the story of an intelligent but poor and unconnected woman who reaches beyond her class or social status in love. She's drawn to a powerful (and sometimes older) man whom she ultimately loves, even though she also resents his power. At first, he doesn't take her seriously because socially she is beneath him or the world he lives in excludes or devalues her. This love story is built around both the attraction and repulsion of unequal power.

She is alone and doesn't feel she belongs anywhere, while he's part of a privileged and large world filled with comfort and helpful connections. He initially discounts her but is finally drawn to her intelligence and character. However, he recognizes her true value and falls in love with her only after she rejects him. Her display of independence assures him that she is not like all the other manipulative or acquisitive women he has known.

The downstairs woman must overcome her fear and resentment of the upstairs man's power. It happens when she sees he's really a good man and that he feels vulnerable too. This is the story of the classic novels *Jane Eyre, Pride and Prejudice*, and *Rebecca*, and contemporary movies like *Pretty Woman*.

This love plot is characterized by misunderstandings and misperceptions that result from lovers trying to communicate across a social divide. The man makes somewhat limited advances that the woman misinterprets as being less, or more, than they actually are. In the happy endings of this story, he overcomes the social obstacles to their union because he's strong enough to make independent judgments and choices. She discovers that he is really sensitive and tender despite his arrogant or intimidating behavior. In real life this is the story of an employee falling in love with her boss, a mistress waiting for her wealthy lover to divorce his wife, an au pair becoming the lady of the house.

Many women drawn to the Upstairs-Downstairs scenario had fathers who criticized or abused them, fathers who made them feel worthless and unprotected. Later in life the downstairs woman is drawn to a romantic scenario that recalls the original rejection because she wants to use the experience to get over her anger or fear of her father. She is looking for a soft and vulnerable heart hidden beneath the man's cold exterior; if she finds this, she will be able to forgive him and receive the love, recognition, and protection she was originally denied. This woman is not attracted to an ordinary "downstairs" man because he would not allow her to replay a scenario in which she wins the love of a man who has great power.

This story also appeals to women with other psychological backgrounds. Women and men are still not treated equally, and many women feel powerless in relationship to men. The story of a woman who can match and be loved by the most powerful man—on the strength of her natural talents and character—is naturally very appealing. All of us love romantic stories about people who discover each other's true character and value beneath their outward appearances. We want to be recognized and loved for who we are as individuals, not for our money or social connections.

The heroine of the Upstairs-Downstairs scenario is socially out of place. She has no family (or only an awful one she needs to escape from). She's a self-made woman who winds up romantically sparring with a man who comes from the landed gentry (or its modern equivalent). She will learn that he also has his own vulnerabilities.

The popular movie *Pretty Woman* is about a prostitute who wins the love of Edward, a handsome and rich businessman. In many ways, the film plot recalls the classic novel *Jane Eyre* by Charlotte Brontë. Jane Eyre is a poor, orphaned governess who eventually marries her employer—Edward Rochester, the intimidating lord of the manor, who is twice her age. She uncovers his tender side and nurses him back to health and happiness after he has been blinded and maimed in a fire that destroys his ancestral property. And in return, he gives her the home, love, and sense of connection she has always wanted.

Daphne du Maurier's novel *Rebecca* (and the Alfred Hitchcock film version, starring Laurence Olivier, Joan Fontaine, and Judith Anderson) is another classic Upstairs-Downstairs plot. But in this love story, the female narrator lacks the independence and spunk that typically characterize heroines in this plot.

In *Rebecca*, the young heroine is timid, mousy, awkward, and anxious. Even though she narrates the story, she is nameless, as a metaphor for her social insignificance—she's a nobody surrounded by rich and important people. Like Jane Eyre, she's an orphan, but since the story is set in 1940 rather than the nineteenth century, she works as a traveling companion and secretary to a rich and obnoxious older woman. While traveling with her employer, she meets the moody and aristocratic widower Maxim de Winter, who has recently lost his beautiful wife, Rebecca, in a boating accident. Drawn to the narrator's youth and innocence, de Winter marries her, and despite (or because of) his remoteness and bad temper, she looks on her new husband with awe.

When they return to Manderlay, her husband's ancestral estate, the heroine finds she cannot fill Rebecca's shoes. Even Rebecca's maid makes her feel like a fraudulent interloper, warning her: "She may be dead, but she's still mistress of this house." At one point, she drops and breaks a small ceramic object in Rebecca's drawing room and is so filled with shame she hides the shards. She's like a small child who's afraid she'll be caught and punished for trespassing.

This story conveys the self-consciousness one kind of downstairs woman might feel around her lover's family and friends. This heroine's husband has at least chosen her (even if sometimes she doubts his love); his associates are far less welcoming. They constantly remind her she doesn't belong.

Eventually, the heroine of *Rebecca* gains strength when she learns that her husband really hated his first wife. Like Jane Eyre, once she realizes the hero is even more vulnerable than she is, she takes command and becomes the more powerful partner in her marriage. When her husband is arrested and tried for the murder of Rebecca, the new Mrs. de Winter is a tower of strength and pulls her husband through the ordeal.

Many interpreters have argued that the endings of *Jane Eyre* and *Rebecca* are symbolic castrations of the rich and powerful husbands. Both heroes are physically maimed or blinded in the fires that destroy their ancestral estates—they not only lose their money and the symbol of their privilege, but they also need to be wheeled around or guided by their wives. But that interpretation is too obvious and misunderstands the heroine's motives. These women do not wish for their partners to be castrated—after all, they were drawn to powerful men. The fires and wounds are the price these men must pay to free themselves from their first wives. The heroines don't want castrated husbands; instead they want to uncover a less frightening and angry side of their partners—and ultimately to be equals in the marriage.

That they wind up with men just as vulnerable as they are may also have other meanings. Their husbands' loss of stature may represent more realistic marital aspirations for downstairs women—not every orphan will marry into the landed gentry. Or perhaps the ending suggests that a downstairs woman will marry wealth only if she accepts serious infirmities in her husband. This may or may not be part of the message, but it's clear that the woman in this scenario evolves from a victim to a victor, and an unequal relationship evens out.

In her essay "Balancing Acts," the literary critic Phyllis Rose also considers the castration question in *Jane Eyre* and modern tales of women who get along better with partners who are seriously maimed (her examples include the movies *Coming Home* and *Belle de Jour*. According to Rose, these heroines don't wish for their mates to be injured, but they find their relationships more satisfying once the balance of power has shifted. As Rose points out, power has always been recognized as a turn-on for women, and this is certainly true in the Upstairs-Downstairs scenario. But less recognized is the woman's desire to be strong herself and to have a partner who isn't always the one in control.

Jane Austen's *Pride and Prejudice* also offers a plot of attraction and repulsion between a heroine who has only a minimal dowry and a wealthy aristocrat. One recent six-part British television adaptation of the novel (with Colin Firth and Jennifer Ehle) drew an audience in England that was so devoted it recalled the popularity of *Masterpiece Theatre's Upstairs Downstairs* of three decades ago.

The story revolves around Elizabeth Bennet, an intelligent middle-class heroine who spars with Mr. Darcy, the rich and arrogant friend of a neighbor. He has offended Elizabeth with his snobbish and dismissive behavior. Despite Darcy's distaste for Elizabeth's vulgar and money-obsessed mother, and his family's objection to her inferior

social rank, he eventually recognizes Elizabeth's superior qualities and
falls in love with her.

At first, Elizabeth misunderstands Darcy and rejects him, which
only makes him want her more because now he is sure she's not just
after his money. Eventually, she realizes he is truly honorable and generous and not the rich villain she thought he was. Despite their different social backgrounds, they see they have found their true match.
Elizabeth becomes the mistress of the grand estate she once admired
from afar, instead of living with her unbearable mother.

The recent movie *You've Got Mail* is usually described as a
remake of *The Shop Around the Corner*. But it also bears a striking
similarity to *Pride and Prejudice* as a romantic scenario. In fact, the
heroine of *You've Got Mail* is always quoting *Pride and Prejudice;* it's
her favorite novel.

Tom Hanks plays Joe Fox, the scion of the family-owned Fox
megabookstore that is driving every small bookshop in Manhattan
out of business. Just around the corner from the new behemoth is a
lovely children's bookstore that has served the neighborhood for
two generations. Meg Ryan plays a woman who inherited this old-
fashioned shop from her mother, and in fact it is all she has left of her
mother, her family, and her childhood. She's not less educated than
Joe Fox, but she is an orphan who is struggling to discover her place
in the world and to keep her shop from going out of business, while
Fox is the rich and powerful new neighbor who at first appears to be
as arrogant as Mr. Darcy.

When Tom Hanks and his megastore threaten her shop, Ryan
stages a public protest, vilifying him in the media. But his juggernaut
store prevails, and Ryan is forced out of business and must fire her
loyal employees (one of whom dates back to her mother's time), who
in many ways have become a surrogate family.

While all this is happening, Ryan is simultaneously falling in love
with an anonymous man she knows only through the Internet—they
have developed a genuine intimacy without ever meeting or reveal-

ing their true social identities. Of course, we know that Tom Hanks is the mystery man. He is the first to discover that his enemy and beloved are the same person, but he keeps his Internet identity a secret. He knows he will never win Ryan's affections until he convinces her that he's really a nice guy even though his business has destroyed hers.

Ryan recognizes the hero's true good nature only after she realizes that closing the store was not the worst thing that could have happened. Since it represented her mother, she couldn't have closed it voluntarily, but once it's gone she is free to pursue her own aspirations—like writing her own books for children. In effect, the only way she can love the right man for her is to give up her attachment to her dead and idealized mother. Like Elizabeth Bennet, she needs a Mr. Darcy in order to be able to move away.

What are these stories really about and which women are drawn to them? The lives of Charlotte Brontë and Jane Eyre—the two great authors who first devised these basic plots—offer important clues. In her book *Dreams of Love and Faithful Encounters,* Ethel Spector Person, a psychoanalyst, has written that Charlotte Brontë wrote the novel *Jane Eyre* as a self-consoling fantasy, to overcome a painful and humiliating romantic rejection. She had felt unrequited love for an older married colleague in the school where she worked, and she'd been fired and sent away when the man's wife became aware of Brontë's infatuation. Brontë's pleading and pathetic letters to the man went unanswered, and her love remained unrequited. But she achieved a happier resolution in the great novel she wrote during this time.

Jane Eyre, her heroine, is a plain but resourceful orphan who falls in love with an older, powerful man who is initially cruel and dismissive of her. But Brontë's alter-ego triumphs over the pain and humiliation that Brontë had personally endured. Rochester declares that it is Jane he really loves and wants to marry, and it is Jane who walks out on Rochester. She returns because she knows he can't live without her. For almost all of her life, Charlotte Brontë was a poor "spinster" (by choice—she turned down two proposals) and never expected to marry after her marriageable years had passed, which in her time was her early twenties. She found love and marriage only months before her death, at age thirty-nine.

Brontë's novel allowed her to rewrite her earlier, unrequited love story and turn it into a victory. Her novel served the same psychological purpose that romantic scenarios offer to most of us—giving us a chance to relive a painful experience and bring it to a happier conclusion.

In *Pride and Prejudice,* Jane Austen also used her fiction to triumph over her romantic disappointments. Austen was the less favored daughter of a clergyman who lacked the funds for the dowry that would have allowed Jane to make a desirable marriage. In their family, Jane's older sister Cassandra was seen as the more attractive and lovable one. With eight children to care for, her mother's attention was limited: after Jane was weaned at the age of three months, she was left in the care of a couple who worked for the Austens and wasn't reunited with her parents for another two years.

Without money, Jane was never a socially appropriate choice for the men who interested her. She did receive marriage proposals, but only from men she feared would bore her. As a result, she remained a "spinster" for all of her life, completely dependent on the handouts of relatives, and forced to live with her parents, who kept moving to new towns where she felt increasingly isolated. She had rich relatives and could closely observe the lifestyle she was excluded from. But in Austen's day, spinsters were viewed as dreaded financial burdens on their families. Jane Austen, perhaps the greatest English novelist of all time, had to live in this dependent and humiliating position. Like many women drawn to the Upstairs-Downstairs plot, Austen was always on the outside, looking in.

As a writer, Austen was also denied recognition during her own life. She was forced to publish all her novels under a pseudonym because it wasn't considered proper for a woman to author such works. Like *Jane Eyre, Pride and Prejudice* might have been a consoling romantic fantasy for its author. In the novel, Austen's heroine, Elizabeth, ridicules women who settle for boring husbands they don't love (rationalizing Jane Austen's own decision). But unlike her creator, Elizabeth triumphs by winning the love of Darcy—the most coveted of all marriageable men. And while Austen was forced to live as a pitied spinster in her parents' little cottage (and had to write her great novels on a small desk in the corner of a noisy room), her heroine becomes the mistress of the grandest, most beautiful country estate. Like Brontë, Austen used her fiction as most of us try to use our own stories of love—to turn powerlessness into victory.

The movies *Pretty Woman* and *You've Got Mail* have broad appeal, and the classic prototypes of these stories have touched readers across two centuries. In real life, these stories resonate to women who also have no place in the world, women who don't feel connected or attached to anyone.

This woman often longs for a man who is out of her reach and she may need to play out her love story primarily in her imagination, as a compensating fantasy, in the same way that it was played out by Jane Austen and Charlotte Brontë. Women who favor this love story usually recognize all they are missing—whether it's the intimacy and comfort of a loving family or the advantages that money and social connections provide. Most of their lives, they have been forced to be spectators of other people's happiness. They have their noses pressed to the window, and they want to come in out of the cold.

Given this desire, why would such a woman fall in love with a man who thinks she is beneath serious consideration? Isn't that just rubbing salt in the wound? This man won't recognize her value, and if he does, he usually won't marry her. The answer lies in her childhood. Many women drawn to this love scenario had fathers who ignored them or showed no affection or approval—fathers who couldn't appreciate their qualities. Some of them had fathers who noticed them but were highly critical. Others had fathers who were depressed, distant, and remote, or even abusive or frightening. Some had fathers, like Jane Austen's, who preferred another daughter. But whatever the form of the rejection, they could never win the love and appreciation of their fathers, no matter how hard they tried. Furthermore, their mothers were typically unable to make up for that damage and neglect—so their fathers' rejection was an unmitigated blow.

Because she never had a relationship with a man who was caring, the "downstairs" woman is trying to reduce her anger and her fear of men, and symbolically, to win the love of her father. For this reason, she isn't drawn to men who choose her. Instead, she keeps reliving the story of winning the love of a man who ignores her or is incapable of appreciating her. She repeats that story not because she wants to be punished but because she wants to move from the role of the victim to the role of the victor. In doing so she becomes recognized and loved. Her wish to overcome her anger and fear of men is the reason why these stories always have heroes with a cold exterior hiding a sensitive and caring soul. The woman needs to change the man into a less frightening figure because she wants to forgive him.

The figure of a cold and rejecting father is obvious in stories like *Jane Eyre* and du Maurier's *Rebecca,* in which the heroines fall in love with men who are twice their age. But even when the hero and heroine are contemporaries, he is a wealthy, important man while she is in a powerless position. And in this way the hero represents patriarchal power. Darcy in *Pride and Prejudice,* Joe Fox in *You've Got Mail,* and Edward, the millionaire in *Pretty Woman,* may not be older than the heroines, but they have the power and wealth of their fathers. They are the heirs to their own rich fathers and share their fathers' power to ignore human need and push other people around.

While it may seem unlikely, the Upstairs-Downstairs love affair is common—at least in relationships and fantasies, if not in matrimony. Millionaires don't often marry hookers, even pretty women, but men do get involved with their secretaries, mistresses, and baby-sitters. The outcomes of these affairs depend on several factors, including the choices the woman makes. In the movies, as in real life, the downstairs woman often wins the powerful man's devotion only after she shows her real inner strength and independence. She needs to let him know she will leave any man who doesn't treat her respectfully—no matter how rich and wealthy he is. Jane Eyre, Elizabeth Bennet, and the heroines of *Pretty Woman* and *You've Got Mail* all rejected their heroes at some point and had to be courted back with a marriage proposal.

An example of how preferred love scenarios may be passed on from one generation to the next is the 1982 film *An Officer and a Gentleman*. Richard Gere plays an ambitious but rebellious young orphan who has virtually raised himself. His mother died when he was a child, and his alcoholic father has never been much of a parent. Gere aspires to become a naval officer and pilot, but with his lower class background, he's out of place at officer training school. Like the heroines of this romantic scenario, he too, is reaching beyond his class—though in his career aspirations rather than in love.

In his transformation from a self-destructive loser, the Gere character is aided by two figures: his tough drill sergeant (Louis Gossett Jr.) and a young woman who comes from a background much like his own. The heroine (Debra Winger) works in a nearby box factory and has been going to dances at the naval training base, hoping to find a desirable husband. The naval trainees are warned that these women will try to snare them with an accidental pregnancy. Indeed, that's the plan of Winger's best friend, who has paired off with one of Gere's buddies.

But Winger, Gere's girlfriend, doesn't stoop to such tactics with Gere. Instead, it's her love and support that pull Gere through his training, and she helps him become a man, as much as the drill sergeant does. But as his tour at the base is concluding, and Gere begins to withdraw from Winger, she shows her independence and dignity.

She walks away and takes up with a new man—actually, a senior flight instructor, a full-fledged officer.

Like the other downstairs heroines, Winger is not blessed with a loving father. Her biological father had also been a naval officer-in-training at the base, who'd left town and abandoned her mother (who also worked in the box factory) when she became pregnant. Winger's only tie to her father is a photograph. Her search for a husband at the naval base is an obvious reenactment of her mother's story, as well as an effort to symbolically win the love of a father who'd treated both her and her mother badly. Winger's mother gives her the strength not to pursue Gere; she tells her that pride is more important.

It's that dignity that wins back the hero. Instead of vanishing, Gere races from his graduation ceremony to claim the woman he loves. Looking like a prince in his white officer's uniform, he drives his motorcycle right up the ramp into the box factory and carries the heroine away. Yes, it's a Hollywood ending, but it accurately shows the importance of self-respect in this story about love and equality.

The Long Climb Upstairs: Carmen Gonzales

Carmen Gonzales grew up in Queens, New York, the youngest of three sisters. Her father was bitterly disappointed when she was born because he'd really wanted a son. His wife's health was poor, so Carmen was the last child they could have, and her father never forgave her for being born. It was easier to hold a grudge against the child than to blame his sick wife.

As far back as Carmen could remember, her father rejected her and made her feel unworthy and unloved. Unlike her sisters and cousins, Carmen kept her nose buried in books, and everyone joked that she didn't really belong to the family. Whenever she tried to get her father's attention, he brushed her off, usually with a derogatory remark about how bad she looked. He was clearly more loving to Carmen's oldest sister, Lucy, who physically resembled Mr. Gonzales

and who hadn't thwarted her father's dream of having a son. As
Carmen moved into her teenage years, she lacked confidence about
her appearance, largely because her father had either mocked or
ignored her.

She poured her energy and ambition into her schoolwork and
did extremely well. But instead of winning her father's approval, Carmen only drew greater hostility. Her success seemed to threaten her
father's self-esteem. Mr. Gonzales earned a decent living as a plumber,
but he had never finished high school, and Carmen's academic success made him feel inadequate; he retaliated by undermining her self-
confidence.

Her mother was too ill to pay Carmen the kind of attention that
might have offset her father's rejection. Also, Mrs. Gonzales thought
that criticizing her husband's cruelty toward her daughter would
make him even angrier. Carmen graduated near the top of her high
school class, and she could have won scholarships to first-rate col-
leges, but no one ever encouraged her to apply. Instead, she attended
college classes at night and worked for the phone company during
the day. Eventually, she earned her credentials as a paralegal worker.
Her work performance was so outstanding that she wound up assist-
ing a highly successful medical malpractice attorney.

Carmen fell in love with her boss, Ken Davis, the first time she
saw him in court. He was mesmerizing—eloquent and passionate in
his defense of children whose lives had been wrecked by negligent
doctors and hospitals.

It was easy for Carmen to identify with this cause and to fight
the powerful authority figures who had inflicted such pain on innocent children. Her passionate sense of injustice on their behalf
rationalized the long hours she put into her work for low wages. It
was obvious that Ken wasn't close to his wife. His family lived in a
beautiful house in Connecticut, and he chose to stay in Manhattan
during the week instead of commuting. This gave him the chance

to pursue casual affairs with an endless series of attractive young women.

Carmen and her boss never had an affair—Ken wasn't especially attracted to her. Mainly, he viewed her as a reliable workhorse he could exploit and depend on. On a few occasions, when they were in the middle of a trial, they had dinner together when they worked until midnight. In these circumstances, Ken often told Carmen how unhappy he was in his marriage, and how his wife and children didn't appreciate him.

Ken was grateful for her dedication to his cases and commended her on her work. When they won a major victory, they celebrated with champagne. Unfortunately, Carmen misinterpreted these shared moments and Ken's disclosures of his marital problems as evidence that Ken preferred to be with her. Her attraction to him got in the way of her usual intelligence.

Carmen's friends at work tried to point out that she was being exploited—she put in eighty hours a week, and was paid for forty. And while Ken and his partners were getting rich on the big settlements and verdicts she helped to win, all Carmen was getting was a pat on the back. What kept her going was the fantasy that one day Ken would realize that she was the woman for him. All of her life, Carmen had been the one who loved rather than the one who was loved because she always picked men who didn't recognize her value.

Her fantasy world collapsed when Ken finally divorced his wife and immediately became seriously involved with an attractive female colleague—a fellow attorney who wasn't particularly nice. Even worse, Ken's new girlfriend regularly asked Carmen to make their reservations for dinner or travel.

At thirty-two, Carmen sank into a deep depression and felt her life was over. An older female attorney, Claire, who also worked at the firm, had seen it all. One night, she took Carmen out and told her what she thought: Ken was attracted to women who presented more of a challenge, and Carmen would never appeal to him as long as she treated him like a god and considered it a blessing to be used by him. In Claire's view, Carmen had only one reasonable choice: she had to leave the firm and get a law degree herself. She was already doing the work of lawyers, and the firm was exploiting her.

Claire admitted she wasn't wild about Ken, but if Carmen really wanted him, she needed to take herself seriously. Then he might or might not take notice of her, but at least she would have taken better care of herself and expanded her options. As her way of thanking Carmen for all she had contributed to the firm, Claire gave her a check to pay for a cram course to prepare for the law school aptitude test.

Carmen was moved to tears because no one had ever encouraged her aspirations. To her great surprise, she got a very high score on the LSAT and was admitted to a first-rate law school in New York, along with financial aid. Ken was shocked at the turn of events and very sorry to see her go—he knew he would never find as good a paralegal again.

In her first year at law school Carmen did so well that by April she was being courted for a summer internship (and future employment) by a pack of prestigious firms. Ken's firm made an offer, along with the rest, but Carmen chose to go with a different offer. In fact, she would be working with the man who was regarded as Ken's equal (or better) as a leading medical malpractice litigator.

When Ken heard the news, he was crushed. He felt hurt and betrayed and imagined that Carmen would teach his rival all the litigating strategies she learned from him. Although he was furious, he called her and asked her to dinner, hoping to change her mind.

A year had passed since they had last seen each other, and Ken was amazed at Carmen's transformation. In fact, he hardly recognized her. She was gorgeous and self-possessed. When he learned that Carmen was dating a hunky twenty-four-year-old law student, he was insanely jealous.

In the past, Carmen had always been so anxious to please Ken that she focused entirely on him—praising him, offering to help him, agreeing with everything he said. All her energy had been directed toward making him feel good. But Ken was not turned on by women who were so simple and direct, so easy for him to have. In the past, he had always been attracted to manipulative and controlling women, and although he was trying very hard now to make a different choice, he remained more attracted to women who could spar with him and who wouldn't roll over and do everything he wanted.

Carmen was no longer eager to please. Like most Jane Austen heroines, she said less than she thought or meant. He couldn't figure her out, and suddenly he found her mystery extremely attractive.

Now Ken was out to win his case with Carmen. At first, Carmen resisted his advances because she didn't want to get hurt again. But when he told her he wanted to marry her, she fell in love with him all over again. She still chose to work for another firm (though not Ken's rival). She had finally achieved equality in her relationship with Ken, and she didn't want to be in a subordinate position in his firm.

What happened to make Ken fall in love with Carmen? For one thing, to appeal to this competitive man, she had to become more of a challenge. Claire was correct. Although he appreciated her sincerity before, he found her more attractive now that he had to fight for her. But most of all, her independence attracted him. His greatest fear was to be taken by another greedy woman who was just after his money. Now that he had to compete for her, he felt more assured that she wasn't just trying to get something from him. He could recognize her value.

Carmen was no longer naive. She had previously refused to see the role that power played in love. Even though power had been an aphrodisiac to her, she hadn't imagined it would be to a man—she had been so locked up in playing the role of the adoring little girl trying to win the love of her rejecting father.

Called to the Big House: Kim Carlson

Kim Carlson's story offers a different version of the Upstairs-Downstairs scenario, this one closer to *Jane Eyre*. Her childhood in a small town in northern Minnesota was not especially happy. Kim's mother worked long hours as a waitress, and her father was fairly withdrawn from the family, so Kim had to care for her four younger siblings. From summer through fall her father was usually out fishing or hunting. In the winter, when it was too cold to leave the house, he just stared at the television, drinking beer until he fell asleep. The kids knew to stay away from him after he'd been drinking. He couldn't handle alcohol and threatened to punch anyone who irritated him.

After finishing high school, Kim got a nursing degree and stayed at home until her youngest sister turned eighteen. She'd become an excellent pediatric nurse, as she had a special gift for working with young children. Now that she'd seen her siblings through high school, she accepted a nursing position at a renowned children's hospital in Boston.

Kim was very pretty (a willowy blonde with startling blue eyes) and naturally warm and caring, so men always wanted to date her. But Kim was shy, a little afraid of men, and usually preferred the company of her roommates.

After she'd been working in Boston for a year, one of the children who came under Kim's care was the seven-year-old son of a wealthy and powerful Boston family. The child, Michael, had been conceived unexpectedly when the Stewarts were middle-aged and their other children were grown. They'd gone ahead with the pregnancy, and Michael was born with severe physical and mental disabilities. Aside from having Down's syndrome, he suffered from many congenital abnormalities, including heart malformations and hearing impairments—problems that required several operations and long periods in the hospital.

Kim established a special bond with Michael, as no one else had, and when it was time for him to leave the hospital, he made a terrible fuss for the first time in his life. The child did not want to part from Kim, and he begged his parents not to take him away from her. Neither of the Stewarts had ever figured out how to relate to their son (all the other Stewarts were exceptional achievers), so in Kim they saw an answer to their problems. They begged her to leave her job and move into their home, where she'd be paid twice her nursing salary and her only responsibility would be to take care of Michael.

Kim was conflicted—she felt sorry for the child and thought she could make a big difference in his life. On the other hand, this job would be far more isolating than her work in the hospital. Her friends and roommates were opposed to the plan. Kim was now twenty-six, and they thought she should be out in the world, where she could meet a suitable husband and have a family of her own. The Stewarts lived in a grand mansion on Chestnut Hill in Brookline—and had a summer home in Maine. But how would Kim meet any men if she became a full-time nanny?

Mrs. Stewart found it unpleasant having Michael at home. She wanted to send him to a "boarding school" for children with severe disabilities, though her husband was opposed to this idea. She saw Kim as the only way she would consider keeping the child at home, and she let Kim know what her decision would mean for the child.

Kim felt sorry for Michael and thought he'd be miserable in an institution. And lately, the shortage of nurses at the hospital was making her job less attractive. She was also really curious about the Stewarts' lives—her own life having been so narrow and her circle of acquaintances so small. The Stewarts were at the center of Boston society, and living with them might broaden her horizons.

When she first saw their house, it reminded her of a palace. Everything about it displayed perfect taste and care. It was a beautiful Victorian mansion, with a grand and dramatic staircase illuminated by a huge stained glass window. Lovely gardens surrounded the house. The Stewarts' bedroom and dressing rooms were on the second floor, as was Michael's suite. Her bedroom was on the third floor, on a corridor of smaller guest rooms, but it was nicer than any room she'd lived in before.

The Stewarts had a maid, a cook, and a gardener-handyman, so Kim's sole responsibility was to care for Michael. She and the child and the other help had the house pretty much to themselves. Mr. Stewart was the director of a large investment firm in downtown Boston, and Mrs. Stewart served on the boards of museums and nonprofit organizations. On weekdays, Mrs. Stewart usually ate dinner with her friends, while her husband worked late and ate at his club. The older children were away from home at school—the daughter was an undergraduate at Yale, and the son was at Harvard Business School.

The first thing Kim did was use her hospital connections to find a few children nearby who shared some of Michael's disabilities. She thought he really needed to play with his peers. Three mornings a week, their parents dropped them off at the Stewarts' where Kim directed a play group. The children's parents were delighted to have a break, and Kim felt she was making a difference in several lives. Within a few months Michael seemed like a different child—a lot happier and more communicative.

David Stewart started coming home for dinner instead of eating at his club. He'd always felt guilty about leaving Michael alone at night, but with his wife rarely at home, he hadn't seen much point in eating at home all alone. Now that Kim was living there, the two of them usually ate together after reading a bedtime story to Michael. At first Kim thought David was distant and intimidating. She'd try to make him laugh about something Michael had said or done that day, but he was moody and austere, and she never knew what response she'd get. He was also such a knowledgeable and powerful man that he frightened her a little.

David noticed how much happier his son was under the care of this warm and beautiful au pair and also realized that Kim had the same effect on him. David's wife had always been cold sexually, and his own sexuality had gone into hibernation. He tried not to let his eyes rest too long on Kim because just being close to her had started to excite him. Seeing Kim's spontaneous affection for his poor little son made his long-suppressed anger toward his wife begin to grow.

After dinner, Kim and David usually sat in the cozy library and talked. Gradually, he got her to tell him about her life, and he told her about his. This became the favorite part of Kim's day—no man had ever shown an interest in her thoughts or observations, except when they were trying to seduce her. Soon she began feeling disappointed at the sound of Mrs. Stewart's Mercedes pulling up in front of the house. That was her cue to say good night and to retire to her room.

One night, in the library, when David drew close to show Kim an illustration from a book about Rembrandt, she noticed that he was breathing heavily and that he had an erection! Her own heart started to beat wildly. She froze, and David turned away. After that, Kim started to have sexual fantasies about him and to imagine herself taking his wife's place.

On Christmas day, the Stewarts always gave a large party, and that year almost two hundred relatives and friends came. Mrs. Stewart didn't want Michael running around the house during the party, so Kim turned the evening into an "overnight" camping trip for Michael and herself on the third floor, complete with a tent and toasting marshmallows in the fireplace.

Late that night, after all the guests had gone, Kim went down to the kitchen to make a cup of tea. As she approached, she heard the Stewarts arguing bitterly, which surprised and excited her. But suddenly, her mood changed when David's raised voice sounded threatening and obviously drunk. The next thing she heard was a loud crash; from her place on the staircase she had seen him pick up a wine bottle and hurl it into the fireplace. Now, afraid of being noticed, she scurried up the stairs, barely missing Mrs. Stewart, who came storming out of the kitchen.

David's drunken anger devastated her. She began to wonder if she had misread him—perhaps he was more like her father than she realized. A few days later David told her that he and his wife were separating. Mrs. Stewart would be staying with a friend in town, and he asked Kim to stay on in the house because Michael needed her now more than ever. She agreed to stay for a while, but she was very nervous. Now she wondered who the real man was—the cold and distant man she had first observed, the kind and gentle man who had slowly emerged in the library, or the violent drunk who hurled bottles at this wife?

It was a while before Kim learned what happened during the fight she'd overheard. David had become a little drunk during the evening, and after the guests had gone, his wife had made a cutting remark. He had fully realized what a cold bitch his wife really was once he saw how differently she and Kim related to Michael. He had long ago given up any hope of his wife being loving toward him, but Kim's care of their son had crystallized the anger he felt toward his wife. He wasn't used to more than one or two drinks, so the alcohol he consumed at the party had removed his inhibitions. He threw the bottle into the fireplace when his wife suggested that Michael was getting too attached to Kim, and that he might be better off in a facility for handicapped children.

The night David told her this, they were sitting beside each other on the sofa. His vulnerability only deepened Kim's attraction to him. Seeing that he could be hurt also made him less intimidating. She reached over to touch him, and instantly, they started to make love. David was in his middle fifties (Kim was twenty-six), so she had wondered whether she would be excited or repelled by his middle-aged body. She was surprised by how ardent a lover he was—and at the strength of her own attraction. She had never felt so sexually drawn to anyone in all her life. David wanted them to marry. It all seemed like a fairy tale coming true.

They kept the relationship to themselves for a while, but soon David's older children picked up the vibes. Their father seemed happy for the first time in their memory, and he looked about twenty years younger. Individually and together, they nagged him to fire Kim, telling him it was unseemly for a man his age to be living in their house with a young girl like that. Annoyed by their selfishness, David told them he had no intention of letting Kim go.

Now the whole family and their friends were bearing down on him. They wanted to know if he'd taken leave of his senses. Couldn't he see that the nanny was a scheming fortune hunter? If he wanted to sleep with her, discreetly, then fine. It would not be the first time a Stewart had sex with the help. But marry her? In their view, she was a totally inappropriate choice. Her background, her age, her lack of sophistication—this was not the type of woman he should have as a wife.

Finally David's children said he could choose between them and his little hooker. They even came to the house when he was at work and told Kim that if she had any genuine feelings for their father and little brother, she would just pack up and leave.

David told Kim that his children's anger was upsetting him. He didn't really care what other people thought, but he didn't want to lose his relationship with his children. His daughter was terribly hurt that he was in love with a woman practically her own age. Although she wasn't fully conscious of her feelings, it made her feel devalued, and she felt her father's love for Kim took away from her special importance to him.

David's son, who had always been closer to his mother, was also furious and threatened never to speak to him again. His parents' separation put him in a confusing position. Now he was his mother's confidant and felt he was replacing his father in his mother's life. At the same time, he didn't want his father getting involved with a woman who was his own age. The separation and the affair somehow placed father and son in the same cohort, and he hated it.

David didn't want to lose his children, so he suggested that he and Kim proceed more slowly until everyone else had calmed down. When her hopes for love had been aroused and fulfilled, Kim had felt that she finally belonged somewhere and to someone, and she felt safe and protected. But now that Kim saw what she was up against, it made her feel that she would never be accepted into this world and would only cause pain to the man she loved. Like Jane Eyre and the hooker in *Pretty Woman* she felt she'd lost the love she'd experienced only briefly. She felt, once again, like an outsider looking in. She realized that David's house could never really be her own home because she could always be asked to leave. With David expressing his doubts, she was feeling alone and insignificant again. She knew she had to leave in a hurry.

By the time David returned from work the next night Kim was packed and ready to go. He was shocked she had taken his suggestion so literally. She explained her decision: even if his children didn't stop speaking to him, they would always resent her. How long would it be before he hated her for causing the rift? How long could he stand to be treated like an old fool by his family and friends? She was leaving because they could never be happy if his children could never accept her.

David had always sacrificed his happiness to do what was expected of him. But thinking of Michael, and all he had learned from Kim's loving attitude toward both of them, he couldn't let her go. He persuaded Kim that she was the only one who cared about his happiness. He was sure that his children would eventually get over their anger, if only because they wouldn't want to lose their inheritance. All his life he'd let others tell him how to live, but now he couldn't imagine living without Kim.

The Stewarts divorced, and Kim and David did marry. Occasionally, Kim worried about the difference in their ages. Now David was a suddenly youthful fifty-five, but she wondered what life would bring in another twenty years, when he was seventy-five and she was forty-six. Then she'd decided to worry about it later. One condition she placed on their marriage was that they would have at least one child together. David wanted to think that he'd still be alive when all of his children completed college, but gradually, the idea of having a child with Kim appealed to him greatly, especially because it would make her so happy. It would be unfair to withhold something so important to her. Also, the child would be financially secure and, most of all, would have a loving mother, which is more than he could say about his own childhood, or that of his children.

Trust Misplaced: The Upstairs Man Folds

We've looked at happy endings to this scenario, but it doesn't always end so well. *Pride and Prejudice, Jane Eyre, Pretty Woman, You've Got Mail,* and the stories of Carmen and Kim all turned out well because the partners were independent and secure enough in their values and judgments to be able to love someone for exactly who they were—including where they had come from, warts and all. This is the key to a happy ending to this story. The heroes were not afraid to marry women who weren't from their crowd—and they admired their lovers for their personal qualities. Even Darcy, who detested Elizabeth's mother, accepted his embarrassing in-laws because they came with Elizabeth and were a part of who she was. Much of his family was just as bad, in their snobbery and arrogance. Carmen accepted Ken, past warts and all, and in *Pretty Woman,* Richard Gere wasn't going to hide the fact that he was marrying an ex-prostitute. In *An Affair to Remember,* the heroine's original fiancé had put her through a five-year finishing course before he felt he could marry her. But this story, when it ends well, is about lovers who have strong, independent characters and fall in love with that quality in others.

Unfortunately, Upstairs-Downstairs stories don't always end this way. A woman who relives the trauma of feeling orphaned because her father didn't value her doesn't always possess the pride to stand up to social exclusion. Even if she does, the man she picks may not have the strength of character she thought he had. He might not be able to accept his beloved exactly as she is—including her family and her past. And often, upstairs men choose lovers their families consider unacceptable as an act of rebellion or separation. But these are not the women they marry.

For example, Angela Silva and John Cutter dated each other exclusively during their last two years of UC Berkeley. Angela came from a Latino working-class family in Sacramento (her father worked in the post office, and her mother worked as a cashier), and John came from a wealthy WASP family from Santa Barbara. At school, no one would have said John was dating down. Angela was so beautiful and was the better student of the two, so most people deemed her the prize to catch. As graduation approached, they planned to stay in the Bay Area to continue their relationship.

John's parents had not been happy with this match all along. They lived within a world of people like themselves. From the first time they met Angela they warned John this would not do—Angela was nice, but in their view her family would always be a huge problem. What would John have in common with them? What could the two families possibly have to say to each other if the pair got married, and heaven forbid, had children? Angela was Catholic, and she would want to raise her children in that faith. They warned John he'd wind up having to take care of her family. Where was this going to end?

Angela's family was also nervous. Her mother was so proud of her daughter, and they knew how hard it must be for her to go to a school where most of the students came from wealthier backgrounds. Her father had always thought she'd be better off going to community college and living at home. They didn't trust the Cutters, and they didn't entirely trust John.

Early in the summer, Angela discovered she was pregnant and told John. Neither of them had intended or wanted this pregnancy, but Angela realized right from the start that she couldn't go through with an abortion. She already felt attached to her baby and just didn't think she could live with destroying it.

John was shocked and then furious with her. They'd been using birth control (condoms), and the pregnancy was no more her fault than his, but even though they had talked in vague terms about the future, they had never agreed to have a child. He also couldn't believe she wanted to have this baby. He thought it was a totally crazy thing to do and that it would wreck his life.

Angela was crushed at John's reaction and realized that going ahead with the pregnancy would mean losing him. But she realized she'd already lost him anyway. Becoming a single mother was not what she'd wished for, but she felt this was her child, and she could not destroy it. She didn't blame John for feeling the way he did—she could see his point of view. But she had to do what was right for her. Her parents weren't pleased, to say the least, but her mother said she would help with the baby.

When John told his parents, they said this was exactly what they had feared. Just what they had expected. The bond he'd felt with Angela vanished into thin air, and he became a boy who needed help from his parents. He accepted their view that she was either crazy or she'd honed in on an opportunity for lifetime support. She'd become the enemy, and they had to come up with a plan. After seeing an attorney, the Cutters persuaded John to offer Angela twenty-five thousand dollars to have an abortion. They'd start with that figure and increase it as much as necessary. John wasn't sure that Angela would go for this plan, but he was so desperate he had to try.

Angela was appalled at the offer. John couldn't buy her off. She was going to do what she thought was right, and the Cutters could keep their precious money. John now decided she was totally crazy, and it worried him terribly that she would have a child who could show up anytime in his life and claim him as a parent. So John begged her never to reveal that he was the father. If she wanted to do this alone, why drag him into it? Angela said she could not make that decision for her child.

Angela was shocked by the things John was saying—his assumption that he could buy her off, that she was in it for the money. He seemed like a total stranger, not the boy she had loved for the past two years. All the time they were together, he had criticized his parents' values and their lifestyle, and now it turned out he was exactly like them.

John had tried, in his limited rebellion, to go beyond his parents' world. But Angela's pregnancy had terrified him. All of a sudden, he felt that his life had gone totally out of his control and that his parents had been wiser all along. What they said suddenly made total sense to him. In addition, not being ready to be a husband or father (that wasn't even up for discussion), he couldn't see himself tied to Angela's family forever. He had once thought she was really nice, but now he decided it must have been just sexual attraction, because they obviously had nothing in common if she could be this crazy.

The thought of the child was his worst nightmare. It would tie him to her entire family for the rest of his life. Now he just felt like a frightened child who needed his parents to protect him from the bad things that could happen in the world.

Eventually Angela had an abortion because her family and friends convinced her that she wasn't in a position to take good care of a child. But she told the Cutters to keep their stinking money. For this, her own father told her she was crazy. Now she was "damaged" he told her, so why shouldn't the Cutters pay? Her mother told her it was okay to refuse the money if it saved her pride.

For several months during this crisis, Angela went through counseling to deal with her guilt and her sadness at the breakup. Finally she recognized that she had misperceived John, and why. She had fallen in love with him because she felt lonely and out of place on the campus. She felt she belonged nowhere: she no longer had much in common with her childhood friends, and she didn't feel at home at UC Berkeley either. John had seemed to be so comfortable there, with his millions of friends and his life in a fraternity house. He knew how to pull all the strings. She'd felt more at home on the campus when she was with him, and she'd viewed him as strong and powerful. But in the end he just seemed like a liar and a user. Unfortunately, the Upstairs-Downstairs scenario often ends this way.

Rejecting Men Who Aren't "Interesting" Enough

Angela's experience isn't the only disappointing ending to this scenario. Many women who are drawn to the Upstairs-Downstairs scenario never marry because the men they fall in love with never marry them, and they are bored by the men who want them. And this is more than just not wanting to be in a club that would let you be a member.

Usually these women fear that life would be unbearable with a man who seems dull and predictable, and they believe they'd be better off alone. Jane Austen also turned down the marriage proposals she received, out of fear that the men would be boring. Elizabeth Bennet, Austen's alter ego in *Pride and Prejudice*, does the same thing, preferring spinsterhood to being trapped with an annoying man. She can't understand why her friend Charlotte chooses a tiresome husband over staying unmarried. This is a common response among downstairs women—who pass up many men who love them on the grounds that those men could never sustain their interest.

But why would boredom seem like the worst fate to this type of person? Of course, an intelligent woman seeks intellectual stimulation and naturally wants a partner whose conversation she enjoys. The women drawn to Upstairs-Downstairs love plots often have highly developed minds, because they often use academic achievement as a way to compensate for a father who fails to appreciate them. They are looking for a man they can admire, and many of them have difficulty admiring a man who isn't their intellectual equal.

But given that downstairs women feel unconnected and alone, why would they give up the chance to have children and a family, out of fear of being bored? Why would boredom appear to be a worse fate than being exploited or treated dismissively? The reasons are not immediately obvious. Surely any selfish partner could seem boring really fast.

Finally, whether a romantic partner seems exciting or boring may depend less on his or her real intellectual endowments than on whether he or she engages us in the scenarios we are trying to set right. A man who doesn't play a role in our primary scenario may strike us as boring—however interesting he may actually be. This is because often there's only one drama that engages us on the deepest emotional level. Of course, this is true for every story of love: when we're addicted to one love story, any lover who doesn't fit into the costarring role is unlikely to engage our interest. But in this love scenario, more than any other, the fear of intellectual boredom is an especially big obstacle to finding a loving mate because women who live out this plot were often made to feel their minds were their only strength. Their intellect is the primary way they have developed self-esteem and related to others.

Remember, the greatest models for this story were created by Jane Austen and Charlotte Brontë, two brilliant women who used fiction to turn their romantic disappointments into victories. They've left a great gift to their readers, and given how talented they were, their work was probably more satisfying to them than the marriages they refused. Many intelligent "downstairs" women wind up living out their love story in their imaginations too. It's lived in their fantasies instead of being put down on paper, in fantasies about relationships that won't take place at all or that won't end the way they want.

SELF-REFLECTIONS

Upstairs-Downstairs love stories can end happily or not, just like all the rest. If you are drawn to this love scenario you need to look at the situation objectively and answer these questions as frankly as possible.

1. Does your partner accept you and where you came from, warts and family and all?

2. Is your partner just rebelling, or does he have the capacity to maintain views and values that are different from those of his family and his friends?

3. Will you need to give up everything you are and have been in order to fit into his life?

4. Is your lover serious about you? Will he marry you, or are you just a woman he finds sexy or interesting, but not the kind of woman with whom he could see raising a family?

5. Does your partner make you feel better about yourself, or does he say things that make you feel unworthy, ashamed, or embarrassed?

6. Are you idealizing your partner while you always feel inferior compared with him? Do you think your lover is superior to you because he grew up with the advantages that money or privilege can provide? Are you undervaluing your own achievements because, after all, you got where you are against the odds, and without much help from anyone? You may not speak five languages like the man you admire, but you arrived in a similar place without all the advantages your partner enjoyed.

7. If the answer to these questions are reasons for concern, you need to figure out where your feelings of inferiority are coming from. Are they coming from within, or does your partner reinforce them? You can change yourself but you probably can't change your partner.

♥

CHAPTER FIVE

Sacrifice:
Guilt Overwhelms Desire

HUMPHREY BOGART: *If that plane leaves the ground and you're not with him, you'll regret it—maybe not today, maybe not tomorrow, but soon, and for the rest of your life.*

INGRID BERGMAN: *But what about us?*

HUMPHREY BOGART: *We'll always have Paris.*

—*Casablanca*

It is a far, far better thing I do, than I have ever done.

—Sydney Carton in *A Tale of Two Cities* by Charles Dickens

David Stewart's conflict between pursuing his own happiness or bowing to his family's wishes is extremely common. But for some people that conflict is the primary scenario. Sacrificing the love of your life for a higher moral purpose or to avoid hurting others is also the theme of some of our most popular romantic movies.

Casablanca, The End of the Affair, The Bridges of Madison County, Brief Encounter, The Horse Whisperer—all of them tell the same story.

A married woman in her thirties or forties, usually with children, unexpectedly begins a passionate, adulterous affair with a soul mate she never expected to meet. He loves her as intensely as she loves him, and he wants her to leave with him. Eventually she must choose between this once-in-a-lifetime happiness and another value: the happiness of her children and husband, or some other serious moral commitment—to God or to her country.

She badly wants to go with her lover, but she fears their union will be so destructive to others it would ultimately poison their own love as well. She believes her guilt would so overwhelm their love that it would be destroyed. The heroine (and often the hero) decides that acting selfishly would make them undeserving of their love.

By sacrificing their relationship, at least they can retain their love in their memories and also know they did the virtuous thing. The sacrifice seems inevitable. In real life, as in literature and movies, this love story usually involves middle-aged people.

People who live out the Sacrifice love plot don't believe they ever could have what they really want without paying a terrible price. And if one of the purposes of romantic love is to raise our self-esteem, this romantic scenario accomplishes that aim, although it's done through renunciation rather than happiness.

The big question is: Why are Sacrifice love stories so popular, when the audience really wants the lovers to be together? And why are the lovers so sure about what they must do? As much as we value personal growth and the pursuit of individual happiness, society also doesn't like lovers who break the web of social obligations and conventions. It's a paradox that some of our most popular love stories link sacrifice with the deepest passion.

The Unconscious Motives and Fears

There's more to this story than appears on the surface. A woman who sacrifices love isn't just being noble; she's reacting to her internal conflicts that make her afraid of choosing love, and these conflicts are caused either by guilt or the fear of losing control, which occurs when we choose passion over a safe, familiar course. The woman who lives out the Sacrifice story is often terrified of feelings that are intense. She has always preferred relationships with tempered emotions. Sometimes both fears—of guilt and of losing control—are present together. But they aren't necessarily connected, and either one is enough to motivate a Sacrifice scenario.

The moral dilemmas that frame the classic Sacrifice stories have evolved over the past fifty years. In the stories written in the 1940s and 1950s, the woman unquestioningly sacrificed her happiness for the welfare of her children and as a way of upholding moral conventions. More recently, the sacrifice isn't taken for granted, and we recognize the price the heroine or hero pays. In the absence of war and guilt over sexuality, the contemporary versions stress the protagonist's responsibility to place the happiness of her children before her own.

In the 1940s and 1950s, sacrificing love for duty was considered the adult thing to do. For example, In *Roman Holiday*, Audrey Hepburn briefly escapes her identity as a princess and heir to the English throne and falls in love with a commoner, played by Gregory Peck. But before long, she remembers her royal obligations and sacrifices her personal happiness to duty. As a result she grows from an unhappy child into a woman who serenely embraces her exalted position.

In *Casablanca*, the duty to fight against the Nazis makes the romantic sacrifice seem just as inevitable. Just when we think Humphrey Bogart and Ingrid Bergman will be reunited, Bogart sacrifices their love (as Bergman had done the last time they parted), announcing that the happiness of two lovers isn't worth a hill of beans compared to their duty to fight for freedom.

As the movie begins, Rick (Bogart) is the cynical owner of a nightclub in World War II Casablanca, when Morocco was an escape route for Europeans fleeing from Nazi-occupied countries. Rick prides himself on "sticking his neck out for nobody." But then into his bar walks Ilsa Lund (Bergman), a woman he loved earlier in Paris. They were planning to escape from Paris together as the Germans were marching in, but with no explanation Ilsa failed to show up at the train station, leaving Rick feeling bitter and abandoned. Now she reappears in Casablanca, the partner of Victor Laszlo, a hero of the French resistance.

Eventually Rick learns that Ilsa really loves him, and that she'd broken her promise to meet him out of concern for his safety and from a sense of duty to the resistance. Seeing him again, she is ready to choose differently, but now Rick must "think for both of them." This time, he's the one who makes the noble sacrifice. As the Nazis close in, he gives Ilsa and Laszlo his two tickets of passage out of danger, instead of leaving with Ilsa himself.

In Paris, believing that he'd been abandoned by Ilsa, Rick had lost the love they once shared. Now that he knows Ilsa always really wanted him, he feels he's regained their love, which he believes will endure in their hearts and memories.

This is a common consolation for people who sacrifice. But why does believing that love will never be forgotten make up for losing love in real life? In Sacrifice stories, the lovers always conclude that keeping their love in their memories is the only way it can remain pure and unspoiled. Believing their love will endure even though they are parting is crucial to their sacrifice. The consolation of being forever missed and loved—of being irreplaceable—allows them to feel important. And that validation addresses the same need the relationship originally sought to fill—the need for recognition and meaning that their lives were not giving them before they met.

Graham Greene's novel *The End of the Affair* and its recent film version take place in World War II London. In the movie, on a dark, rainy night a government official named Henry Miles (played by Stephen Rea) and a novelist named Maurice Bendix (played by Ralph Fiennes) meet in a park. Henry tells Maurice that he fears his wife Sarah (Julianne Moore) is having an affair, not realizing that Sarah had once been Maurice's lover. Sarah had left Maurice a bitter man after mysteriously withdrawing from their passionate relationship two years earlier. Henry questions Maurice about finding a private detective. But now Maurice is insanely jealous that Sarah apparently has a new lover, and he arranges on his own for her to be followed.

Eventually we learn that Sarah is actually dying. Her secret trysts are with a priest, not a new lover. She needs to deal with the guilt she feels about her adulterous love for Maurice. Maurice also finally learns why she broke off the affair. They had been making love when a bomb exploded, blasting Maurice into the air. After the explosion, Maurice appeared to be dead, and Sarah dropped to her knees and made a desperate pact with God. She vowed that if Maurice were restored to life, she would renounce the adulterous affair. To Sarah's amazement, Maurice then stood up (saying he'd only been knocked unconscious).

Now she had to keep her bargain with God and live without the love that had given meaning to her life. She merely told Maurice that they could no longer be lovers, but their love wouldn't stop just because they could no longer see each other. The end of their affair would not be the end of their love. But Maurice was baffled and devastated, not understanding how his lover could suddenly abandon him with no explanation.

In this Sacrifice story, guilt is behind the renunciation of love. The heroine's Catholic faith had once been the only source of meaning she needed, but she had lost that faith. Guilt has kept her in a loveless marriage. Her love for Maurice had filled the void left by the loss of her religious convictions. When God answered her prayers during the episode with the bomb her faith was restored, but the price was sacrificing her lover. Her overpowering guilt led to the end of the affair; only religious faith relieved it.

Another story of romantic sacrifice is found in the classic film

Brief Encounter. Set in postwar England, it was written about the same period as *Casablanca* and Greene's novel *The End of the Affair.* A seemingly happy wife and mother accidentally meets a married physician while waiting for a train. They are immediately drawn to each other, and surreptitiously begin falling in love. They have the kind of conversations the heroine has never had with her husband. But at a critical juncture, she realizes she can't leave her family. After they agree to part and her lover leaves for Africa, the heroine is momentarily tempted to throw herself in front of a train. Instead, she collects herself, goes home, and picks up her life as it was before.

Renouncing Passion

This classic story is updated in Robert James Waller's novel *The Bridges of Madison County,* one of the all-time best-selling novels in America. It was also made into a movie starring Clint Eastwood and Meryl Streep. The novel drew a huge and devoted audience that kept it alive with "Bridges" fan clubs.

In the movie version, which is somewhat different than the novel, the story of *The Bridges of Madison County* is told retrospectively, through the heroine's journals and a letter to her adult children, which they are given to read only after her death. Francesca (Meryl Streep in the movie) came from Italy after World War II to live on a farm in Iowa with her American husband. The story opens as her middle-aged children have returned to bury Francesca beside their father. But they learn from her letter that she wants to be cremated and to have her ashes tossed from a nearby covered bridge. She goes on to tell them who she really was—about the love she sacrificed for them, and the four most important days of her life.

The scene dissolves to twenty years earlier, and the story is told from Francesca's point of view. She loves her family, but they are so caught up in their own lives they barely notice her. There is never any meaningful conversation at the dinner table.

One summer, Francesca's husband and children leave home for several days to attend a fair. On her first morning alone, a truck pulls up to her house. A handsome stranger is lost and needs directions. It is Robert Kincaid (Clint Eastwood), a photographer sent by *National Geographic* to photograph the county's covered bridges. Kincaid is attentive and sexy—he's the first person who has really noticed Francesca in many years. They have an instantaneous rapport and become lovers.

Robert has always followed his desires, and he wants Francesca to leave with him. Francesca explains that a mother can't just do what she wants. She needs to remain fixed and unchanged for her children.

Robert insists they were meant to be together, and they won't have this chance for happiness again. At one point, Francesca even packs her suitcase, because she's really dying to go. But at the critical moment, she can't. She fears it would destroy her decent husband and would undermine everything she has taught her children about family and fidelity.

Like most of the protagonists of Sacrifice love plots, she fears that leaving would cause her to feel overwhelming guilt. Soon she would blame Robert and their love for damaging others. Like Rick in *Casablanca,* she decides that the only way to preserve that love is to hold it in her memory.

After a final dramatic scene of renunciation, Francesca and Robert never meet again. But decades later, when she is a widow, Francesca receives a letter and package forwarded by an attorney. She learns Robert has died and that he never stopped loving her. His last wish was to be cremated and have his ashes scattered from the bridge where they first fell in love. When her own death approaches, she decides that she wants her ashes to follow Robert's, and she doesn't want the story of her love and her sacrifice to go with her to the grave.

As in *Casablanca* and *The End of the Affair,* the lovers in this Sacrifice scenario are faithful to each other—retaining their love until the end of their lives in memory, which is the only place they permitted it to exist.

Francesca's children are shocked by these revelations, and her son, especially, is furious. "I feel like she cheated on me," he declares, responding much like David Stewart's daughter. His mother's passion for a lover makes him feel less loved as a child. But Francesca's daughter soon recognizes how deeply her mother's secret has shaped her own life. For twenty years, the daughter had stayed in a miserable marriage because her mother's example had taught her that a woman doesn't leave. Seeing how much her mother's sacrifice has shaped both their lives, she finds the courage to call her husband and ask for a divorce.

The Price of Sacrifice

Though Francesca's sacrifice seems inevitable, considering when and where she lived, the retelling in the 1980s highlights what she lost in that choice and raises the question of whether she really did her children a favor. It also points out the change in how we weigh personal happiness against family obligations. But sometimes the choices that parents make are not bound by time but pass down through the generations.

If Francesca had felt that she deserved to claim happiness for herself, she might have conveyed that message to her children as well. She stayed with her husband to avoid wrecking her children's faith in marriage and commitment. But in hindsight, her sacrifice had communicated something unintended—that happiness is not to be found in marriage, and that they shouldn't expect or demand it.

Why did Francesca reveal her secret after her death? Ostensibly, she wanted her bodily remains to wind up next to the right man. Presumably, she also wasn't blind to her children's marriages, and she might have believed that revealing the feelings she'd hidden all her life would give them some wisdom and direction.

But there's more to her telling her secret so late. In fact, it's probably impossible and inhuman to make a huge sacrifice without letting it become known. People who take comfort in being virtuous rather than being happy usually want their virtue acknowledged and recognized, no matter how noble they are. There are limits to anyone's generosity, and few people can wait until after their death to collect their due. Just recall any time you made a sacrifice and failed to ask for what you wanted and deserved. Some degree of resentment usually lingers on.

The Appeal of the Story

What kind of person is drawn to the Sacrifice story? *The Bridges of Madison County* appealed to an audience wider than people who fantasize about running out on their families. This kind of story appeals to people who feel they are missing something important but who are too afraid of rocking the boat. It appeals to the fantasy that everyone has a perfect romantic partner, an erotic and intellectual soul mate—even if we'd have to resist the temptation if he ever showed up. The renunciation raises the romantic and erotic fantasy to a higher spiritual level and removes any guilt. The sacrifice makes the romantic and erotic fantasy acceptable to women (and men) who would never consider leaving their families but who secretly long for more than they have. Obviously, many people feel they've made sacrifices in order to stay loyal to the commitments they made. This story validates their longings for more without arousing their guilt.

The screenplay for *Bridges* was written by Richard LaGravenese, who also wrote the film adaptation of *The Horse Whisperer*. In many ways, it's a contemporary version of the same plot.

Annie MacLean (Kristin Scott Thomas) is the powerful workaholic chief editor of a New York celebrity magazine. She is married to a lawyer and has a fourteen-year-old daughter. Her child, Grace, is badly wounded in a tragic horseback riding accident in which a skidding truck kills her best friend and mutilates her beloved horse, Pilgrim. Grace loses one of her legs, which had to be amputated to save her life.

When Grace sinks into a dangerous depression, Annie fears for her life. Grace agrees with Pilgrim's caretakers that the horse should be put out of his misery and shot; she thinks the same should be done to her. Desperate to save her, Annie tracks down a "horse whisperer" named Tom Booker (Robert Redford) who lives in Montana. Booker is renowned for healing wounded horses. Annie believes that if Pilgrim can be saved, her daughter might also recover.

Booker heals the horse and pulls Grace out of her depression. He and Annie also fall in love, and it's the first time she has felt this kind of passion. When Grace notices what's going on between them, her buried emotions and fears surface, and she falls apart. Not only would the breakup of her family be difficult, but seeing the passion arise between Booker and her beautiful mother uncorks her deeper despair over her damaged appearance and her doubts she will ever be loved. She had never felt she measured up to her mother, and now she feels doomed.

Annie realizes she can't break up her family to pursue her own happiness. Her daughter is too fragile, and Grace's needs must come before her own. She leaves her lover and returns to New York and her husband.

Annie exemplifies a common trait of women drawn to Sacrifice love plots. While some sacrifice their love because of guilt, others exert tight control in their lives. In fact, the main reason they have never before loved passionately is that intense emotions can't be controlled and would make them feel extremely anxious. They have always been in control, which usually means being with a man who either lets them have the upper hand or who doesn't demand too much intimacy or intense emotions. The husbands in *Brief Encounter* and *Bridges of Madison County* hardly notice their wives' emotions.

The controlled woman has always avoided putting all her eggs in one emotional basket. When she does encounter passion, it makes her too anxious to choose it. Her unconscious fear of losing control is expressed by her conscious fear that something terrible will happen if she's ruled by passion. In Annie's case, her daughter's needs are unde-niable, and there is only one reasonable choice. But in less clear-cut circumstances women like Annie often say they must renounce pas-sion in order to avoid damaging others, when they are really moti-vated by a fear of emotions they can't control.

Anna Karenina: A Cautionary Tale

The Sacrifice lover has typically embedded her marriage in a rich social context; this is part of her overall strategy of spreading around her emotional investments. Leaving that world for a passionate love usually means cutting herself off from the entire social network that made her comfortable. She worries that if her new love is not sup-ported and surrounded by that social context, it might become too intense, too solitary and claustrophobic. She might end up totally iso-lated and cut off from her world and her family. In other words, she might wind up like the tragic heroine Anna Karenina.

In Tolstoy's great nineteenth-century novel, Anna Karenina leaves the security of her marriage and loses her young son because she can't resist a passionate love with the handsome officer Count Vron-sky. At first, she gets pleasure from this new kind of love, but soon her total exclusion from society and the loss of her child leave her iso-lated, guilty, and completely dependent on her lover. With only Vron-sky in her life, she begins to behave in the classic manner of the obsessive lover. She's consumed with suspicion and jealousy, and feels certain he will abandon her. She tries to control his movements, and she demands more than he wants to give.

There are in fact grounds for her fears: Vronsky begins to resent the sacrifices he has made for her (especially his military career). But his life isn't nearly so constrained or permanently damaged as Anna's. Vronsky goes out into society and sees other people, though this means leaving her alone. He's not dependent on her in the same way. Eventually, he grows tired of his confined life with Anna and weary of her jealous accusations. Finally he tells her he's joined his old army unit and is going off to war with his friends. They argue, he leaves, and Anna writes him a letter begging to see him before he departs. When she doesn't get a response, she sees only one way out: she kills herself by throwing herself before a train.

This obsessional involvement and desperation are precisely what the Sacrifice woman dreads. She also can't imagine living without her family and the social world that provide her identity and sense of purpose.

Passion and Competing with Your Child

In *The Horse Whisperer*, the hero has a profound impact on the emotionally guarded Annie. She relaxes control, and for the first time in her life she seems willing to leave her busy New York life and live more simply in the mountains with her lover. But finally she is saved from having to make a choice because her daughter's happiness must come first.

In contrast, in *Damage*, a doctor and member of Parliament has been happily living a controlled existence until his son falls in love, and he becomes his son's romantic rival. His jealousy leads him down a path that ends in his son's death. Annie, on the other hand, recognizes that her daughter needs to be the focus of her life. If Annie didn't sacrifice her lover it would only make her daughter feel more envious, defeated, abandoned, and undesirable. The passionate choice is hardly ever the viable option in the telling of these stories. The price always appears to be far too high—even if the sense of danger really stems from a fear of feelings that can't be controlled.

Parents rarely have affairs with their children's partners, but it's not uncommon for middle-aged parents to fall suddenly in love when their children begin to experience romantic love themselves. Rivalry isn't necessarily the motive. Just seeing their child's excitement and joy not only reminds them of what is missing in their own life, but also makes them aware that time is passing. Together, these circumstances often break down the inhibitions that have kept the parent from choosing a passionate relationship before. Sometimes the adolescent who is drawn to very intense affairs is also responding to an unconscious message from their emotionally controlled parents: don't do as I did, follow your heart. Other children who get mixed messages may wind up with conflicting impulses (like their parent) and oscillate between looking for safety and yearning for excitement.

Passing the Conflict to a Child

Mari Matsuyama's pattern was to leave boyfriends who wanted her more than she wanted them. This helped her feel more in control. But she also believes her "split personality" has prevented her from making a satisfying choice. She is now thirty-one and recalls a lover who made her take an uncharacteristic risk.

"I had been in a stable relationship for five years with a guy from my hometown in Connecticut. He was in dental school and he wasn't exciting, but he was stable and secure. I did like the stability and routine, but occasionally, I'd have affairs behind his back. Those affairs were more exciting and intense because of the danger of getting caught. I think I was looking for someone to complete me and take me away to a more exciting life, because my own life was so boring. My long-term boyfriend was not going to do that."

Then Mari met Patrick, a professional tour guide who leads vacation expeditions in Central America.

"I quit my job and left my five-year boyfriend in Connecticut to be with Patrick in Los Angeles, for the excitement. Originally, I went with him because I thought we would take a trip around the world and then come back and get married and have children. He was easygoing and comfortable and relaxed. I tend to be more tense and upset. He was happy-go-lucky. I thought he had all the elements to complete me and give me an exciting life. I was in Los Angeles, without any friends or family, and I looked to Patrick for everything—and he was not there for me. I was very needy. I really needed to be close to Patrick, and he started to pull away. Finally, he bailed out on me, and I wound up traveling alone—not with Patrick. I learned excitement will only take you so far."

Mari didn't have a husband or children, so it was easier for her to take an uncharacteristic risk. In the past, she had peppered her safe and secure life with risky and exciting brief affairs. When she gave up that security to live with a more exciting lover she made the error of thinking that her boyfriend could be her entire world. Without friends or family, she was too dependent on Patrick.

Men who like adventure and excitement usually want a partner who is equally independent. They don't want someone who ties them down like a ball and chain. Mari was somewhat passive when she began her relationship with Patrick, feeling that she needed him to carry her away to a more exciting life.

Alone in a strange city, Mari had only Patrick. The lesson of this story is that you must not expect an exciting lover to fill all your needs. If you do, he'll start seeing you as an albatross around his neck, just as Anna Karenina increasingly appeared to Vronsky.

Weighing the Choice: Ellen Stein

All the classic features of the Sacrifice scenario came into play for Ellen Stein, who is in her early forties and lives in the Chicago suburbs. She's a mother of three children, ages eight to seventeen. Her husband, a businessman, is never at home, and for years he's been having affairs. He rarely has dinner with the family, and he and Ellen have not had sex for years. Ellen had always put up with this arrangement in order to maintain her family. She thought that by trying hard enough, she'd win him back—and keep her family intact.

Ellen had loving parents who placed a strong value on family;

they viewed it as the most important thing in life because earlier they had lived through many traumatic relocations. Ellen had a happy childhood, but her parents died relatively young, and her belief in the sanctity and integrity of the family was one of the few ways she felt connected to her past and the family that raised her.

At age forty-two, Ellen started her first and only extramarital affair. She fell madly in love for the first time in her life, with someone who was an unlikely choice: Daniel was her daughter's piano teacher. He was ten years younger than Ellen, and unlike her husband, money meant little to him. He also made Ellen feel sexy and beautiful, and he liked being around her children.

He wanted Ellen to divorce and to marry him, and to be a good surrogate father for her children. Money wasn't really an obstacle for Ellen because she had enough money of her own to know that her children wouldn't suffer economically. But she was convinced that getting a divorce would cause so much havoc and pain, and be so socially unacceptable, that she felt she must end her love affair and work on her marriage. At first she was tempted to get a divorce, but when she confided in her two sisters they reinforced her fears.

No loving parent wants to inflict pain on her children, and most children want their parents to stay together. As Francesca explained in the movie version of *The Bridges of Madison County*, children want their needs to be primary and they want their parents to remain frozen in time. Parents like Ellen assume that their decisions should always be determined by what is best for their children, and not by what's best for them.

But there was more to Ellen's sacrifice than she was willing to acknowledge. Ellen was brought up to be sensible, conventional, and to do everything in a measured way. She was not accustomed to intense relationships and was terrified of a love that would separate her from the social contexts of her life—her sisters and friends, and the social circles she belonged to with her husband.

If she married Daniel, their love would fall outside the world she'd always lived in. She feared that no social place would support their love. Apart from her children, there would be no boundaries or limits to her romantic attachment; the couple would have only each other. And she worried that her children would be harmed, or that they might never forgive her. She wondered what would happen to them when they visited their father. Would they be exposed to a series of his girlfriends, and who would they be? Would their father even be around when they came to visit?

These are not idle fears, and they don't just come from a cautious disposition. All around us, we get messages about the dangers of passion. Despite all the romantic movies that end happily when the hero and heroine take a chance on love, society generally doesn't approve of going for intense passions over routine ones that fit into social networks. Ellen was being realistic by expecting tremendous disapproval if she left her husband for her lover. But her fear was also personal; she'd always been taught to be careful and conservative.

Being an introspective person, she also questioned her own motivations. Her affair occurred shortly after her oldest daughter had experienced her own first love. She remembers being a little jealous about her daughter's excitement. So she wondered whether her passion for Daniel was actually a way of competing with her own child. Ellen was nothing like the father in *Damage,* who had an affair with his daughter-in-law. But this is an important question for any parent to ask. As we see our children entering the prime of their lives just as we are leaving it, it's natural to feel some envy, and it shouldn't be confused with genuine love.

Ellen also had no way of knowing how the divorce would affect her children. If she divorced, her children would probably be angry and might be exposed to their father's anger as well. But sometimes these fears are greatly exaggerated.

Realistically, would they really never speak to Ellen again or be permanently damaged? The impact of each divorce is different, but children can always find reasons to be angry with their parents, and many do forgive their parents for having the courage to choose passion. And because parents who sacrifice love communicate mixed messages to their children—to be cautious on the one hand, to go for happiness on the other—it's difficult to know or control exactly what message is being sent, or what is being perceived.

Sometimes children of parents like Ellen and her husband—couples who are cool and remote—often act out the choices their parents relinquished. They may engage in reckless or dangerously intense first loves. And those reactions may spur one of the parents to express a new openness to passion.

The impact of a teenager's passion on his parents is one of the themes of Scott Spencer's novel *Endless Love*. The young narrator goes to such extremes to hold on to his first love that he winds up spending ten years in a mental hospital rather than giving up his dream. But even with that terrifying outcome, David Axelrod's father is so shaken by the passion of his son that the emptiness of his own thirty-year marriage becomes intolerable. Mr. Axelrod had always been in love with his wife, but she had never returned those feelings. After watching his son give up everything for love, he regrets all the passion he's missed. When a second chance for love comes along, unexpectedly late in life, Mr. Axelrod is ready to grab it. The novel tells a story of children who are unconsciously programmed to act out what their parents were afraid to do—and sometimes the children are put in danger, because they are really acting out someone else's dream. This is why it's not always clear what is best for the children.

A woman in Ellen Stein's position must also ask herself, honestly, if she can be happy if her love distances her from a world she's always needed. With all romantic choices, we must look at things objectively, no matter how difficult and painful that is. Perhaps her social world is no longer as attractive to her as she thought. She might discover that the sacrifice wasn't worth it—because no one within that world was treating her with that much care. But if she decides to take a chance on love, it would be wise for her to keep those relationships that were gratifying, as well as build up a new world around her new love. Otherwise she might end up like Anna Karenina or Mari Matsuyama, who both destroyed their passionate relationships because they became exclusively dependent on them.

Although children are unhappy when their parents divorce, they also suffer when their parents are in marriages filled with tension and anger. How does a person like Ellen make the best choice? The person caught between desire and convention must ask herself if her fears are exaggerated—but she must also realize that a choice must be made without knowing exactly how things will turn out. It will probably take time for things to settle, and no one should expect their children to forgive them immediately. Still, most children eventually forgive their parents if their parents have treated them in a loving way.

Refusing to Sacrifice: The Price

In the movie *Twice in a Lifetime* the question of whether his children will forgive him is the big one facing the mill worker played by Gene Hackman. On the surface, his twenty-five-year-old marriage seems happy, but it's really emotionally and sexually dead. On his fiftieth birthday, he celebrates with his friends at the local bar while his wife (Ellen Burstyn) stays at home. That night, Hackman meets a waitress (Ann-Margret), an attractive widow who makes him feel alive. In time, the two fall in love. At first Hackman tries to maintain both relationships, because he doesn't want to hurt his wife and anger his three (grown) children, who are very dear to him. But his lover reminds him he can't live two lives and that he's got to make a choice.

Hackman decides to leave his marriage. At first his wife is stunned, then she pulls herself together and starts to build a new life. But of Hackman's three children only his son is sympathetic and glad to see that his father is happy. He tells his father it's okay—that he waited until all the children were grown, so now he deserves a chance to enjoy his life. Hackman's youngest daughter, a sweet and happy

young woman who is getting married herself, is also inclined to forgive him, although she feels her mother needs more of her support.
Most of the fury directed at Hackman comes from his oldest daughter,
who is probably angry for other reasons. She's having marital problems of her own because her husband can't find a job. Her father's
decision to leave his marriage behind is especially threatening to her.

There's a very sad scene at the end when Hackman is treated as
an unwelcome guest at his youngest daughter's wedding. He's not
even invited to the reception at the family's home, on the grounds
that his presence would make his wife too uncomfortable. While
waiting for the newlyweds to emerge from the church, his overtures
to his oldest daughter are loudly and publicly rejected. Suddenly he's
standing alone, in the front of the church, after everyone has left for
the party. It's a bittersweet ending, but he picks up a bunch of flowers to take home to his lover, and as he turns the corner, there's a
spring to his step.

In *Twice in a Lifetime* money is scarce for all the protagonists, and
Hackman gives what little he has to his ex-wife. Obviously, money
plays a large role in many decisions to stay or to go. Perhaps what
stops most people today from leaving a dead marriage for a more passionate love is financial anxiety rather than guilt or fear of doing
irreparable harm. But by the same cynical calculation, departing partners who have any money may take some reassurance from the
thought that their children will eventually come around, if only to
keep from losing their inheritance.

David Stewart, the investment banker who left his wife for
his young nanny, probably knew his older children would ultimately
forgive him because they didn't want to lose his estate. In fact,
he strongly suspected that Kim's youth bothered them less than
their fear that she would inherit his wealth. David Stewart's story
also reminds us that each lover in a relationship is living out his
own romantic scenario. While Kim was immersed in an Upstairs-
Downstairs plot, David was grappling with the Sacrifice scenario.

SELF-REFLECTIONS

If you are caught up in a Sacrifice scenario you need to take an unflinching look at these considerations.

1. We have to make choices in life without knowing exactly how things will turn out.

2. You need to be sure your unexpected passion isn't motivated by envy of your children's youth.

3. If you feel you must sacrifice a true love because you don't want to hurt someone else, then you need to ask whether your fears are exaggerated or whether you'd be uncomfortable in a relationship that's so emotionally intense. You also need to examine the social worlds you may lose if you choose passion over security. Were they really giving you pleasure? Can you find new relationships to take their place?

4. Your children need you tremendously and often their needs must come first. But you have a right to happiness too. Claiming a right to be happy is not a bad thing to be teaching your children either.

CHAPTER SIX

♥

Rescue:
Doing What Your Mother
Could Not

O love, thy kiss would wake the dead!

—ALFRED, LORD TENNYSON, "The Day-Dream"

Rescue seems to play a role in every romantic scenario. In a way, all happy lovers feel that they've been saved. They believe that love has brought out the best in them and that it has given them a much better life. But for some people, Rescue is the central theme or attraction in the relationship, and it is the glue that keeps lovers bonded. Like all the other love stories, Rescue is a reenactment of an earlier, unresolved scenario. It ends with a happier resolution, or it merely repeats the original trauma.

The basic Rescue story is simple: a woman (or man) falls in love with someone who was wounded in the past. In her eyes, her beloved has great potential, but no one has ever given him the care and affection he needed to become his best self. She believes her love can restore him to health or to his full human potential. Furthermore, and this is her ultimate wish, she believes that once she saves him, he will rescue her back. He will be the perfect husband and father, and will give her the protection she missed in childhood. Many of us are raised from childhood with this view of love: think of the lasting appeal of *Beauty and the Beast.*

Unlike the women drawn to powerful but rejecting men, as in the Upstairs-Downstairs scenario, the woman who lives out the Rescue story often had a father she liked and lost when she was young. In some cases, her father didn't actually die of an illness, but he was never allowed to become whole. Either physically or emotionally, he got messed up in life. He may have even been an alcoholic, or abusive, or divorced her mother and left the family. Whatever the circumstances linked to his wounds, the daughter consciously or unconsciously sees her father as the victim.

Often she blames her mother for what happened to her father, even though she's usually not aware of assigning that blame. Sometimes she even blames herself. And in addition to losing her father, she's often called upon to care for her mother or become a surrogate partner. She learns from a young age that it's her job to save the needy.

In adulthood, she falls in love with a man she perceives as wounded, but unconsciously she is reliving the trauma of her youth—hoping, of course, to make it all come out better. If she's able to save or restore her lover, she will have achieved two huge victories: symbolically resurrecting her father so that he can give her the care and protection she missed as a child; and separating from her mother and proving that they are different.

The wounded man she loves is not merely a prince in disguise, someone with untapped potential. He also represents her father because she has imposed her memories and feelings for him on her lover. She sees in her lover the projection or reflection of her father, and the two are always tied together in her unconscious mind. For example, in *Beauty and the Beast,* the heroine runs back and forth between her father and the beast—trying to save one while the other is dying. In the recent movie *Run Lola Run*, the heroine's boyfriend will be killed by gangsters in twenty minutes if she can't raise enough money to save him. Her efforts are repeated three times in nearly identical scenarios that begin the same way but take different turns. Only in the third version is she successful. This time she makes better choices and corrects her mistakes. As a result, she wins the money on her own, resuscitates her father from the brink of death, and her boyfriend becomes a stronger man. The movie illustrates that we may need to reenact our story a few times to bring it to a happy conclusion.

But why does a woman want to rescue a man? Ultimately she wants to be rescued herself. She wants to nurse a man back to health so that he can become the perfect father-husband. Men also fall in love with women they want to rescue—but their motivation is often different. Some men who are drawn to Rescue scenarios are more sexually attracted to weak or injured women than they are to strong women. To them, a weak woman won't threaten their sense of masculinity or potency. Many of these men also had absent or wounded fathers, and they were forced as children to rescue their needy and dependent mothers. As adults, they're attracted to injured women because it's a recapitulation of their childhood and because a weak woman won't make them feel inadequate, as they did as little boys, trying to make their mothers happy. Sometimes when the wounded partner of a male rescuer is healed, the man finds her less sexually alluring. Now that she's stronger, his masculinity is threatened. In contrast, most female rescuers want their partners to recover; when this occurs, the woman proves that she could do what her mother could not.

Restoring her father and outdoing her mother are the primary themes of the Rescue scenario. But this story also has subsidiary themes that stem from the original drama.

Though rescuers are angry with their mothers, they also feel guilty about leaving them. In her remarkable memoir, *Fierce Attachments,* Vivian Gornick has described her mother's smothering grief after Vivian's father died when she was thirteen years old. For a year, her mother forced Vivian to sleep with her because her mother couldn't bear to sleep alone. Every time Vivian tried to escape her mother's embrace and move away toward the wall, her mother would pull her back again. Much as she tries to escape her mother, Vivian is always fiercely attached to her, not only because of the force of her mother's personality, but also because of her overwhelming childhood losses. A child like this is deprived of protection from both parents: her father is dead, and she's the one who has to care for her mother. Gornick does not see herself as a rescuer of men, but she shares with rescuers a common childhood trauma and she chooses troubled partners. She also observes that in her relationships with men, she's less belligerent and more desirous when the man appears to her as weak.

In her adult life, the rescuer often picks a man who needs help and is likely to be dependent on her. This serves two purposes: she won't lose him because he's less likely to leave her, and his dependence also gives her a sense of control, which she badly needs. She and her partner may also have a ferocious bond modeled on her relationship with her mother, one in which she has to sacrifice herself to comfort her lover. This is also why many women can't extricate themselves from partners who turn out to be too wounded. The woman can't leave her injured partner any more than she could leave her mother. Not only is she committed to saving her surrogate father, but she's also never learned to separate from her mother. Her partner comes to represent an amalgam of both parents who need to be saved.

Recall Vicki Lewis (from chapter 2) whose father died when she was young, and who fell in love with an admired male mentor in order to escape her mother, whom she'd cared for since childhood. Vicki thought she was getting into a Pygmalion scenario, but wound up having to rescue her older husband, who was supposed to parent her. On a conscious level, she chose him because she thought he'd be the father she never had. Unconsciously, she was also rescuing her father and her mother.

A selfless devotion to the wounded partner is typical of the most extreme Rescue scenarios. The rescuer refuses to accept that a situation is hopeless, that a partner is never going to get better. Her sense of duty and loyalty to her partner won't allow her to save herself. She needs to show this unwavering loyalty in order to prove she is "good."

Then there are partners who are forced into a Rescue role they didn't choose in the first place (for example, spouses of people who become very ill). They will only play their part reluctantly. If someone tries to coax a nonrescuer into a part that is not in his or her repertoire, the nonrescuer will only go through the motions and give a halfhearted performance. Usually they'll look for someone else to rescue *them* from a situation they regard as unfair. Of course, this is true of all scenarios. Partners don't always cooperate with playing the parts they are assigned.

Some self-help books and organizations view the Rescue scenario as an unhealthy addiction. But this negative image of Rescue focuses only on the most extreme and destructive scenarios—the woman who wastes her life by trying to rehabilitate a hopeless or abusive alcoholic, and the woman who "loves too much." Or the "codependent" woman who needs a weak man in order to feel in control. The critics of rescue relationships also make the error of confusing the psychological origins of this scenario with the problems of people who suffer from romantic obsessions.

In both Obsessive love and Rescue the lover is often unable to give up a relationship that is painful and abusive. Perhaps that's why these two very different scenarios are often confused. In both cases, the lover has felt a deep loss regarding a parent. A child who feels abandoned will do almost anything to get her parent back. She'll take a solemn vow to be good and will never give up trying. All of this is in the hopes of bringing back the parent. That kind of unremitting effort, without any reasonable hope or reward, is often seen in both Rescue and Obsessive scenarios.

Except for this, the two scenarios are very different. Obsessive lovers are dominated by extreme anger and are trying to undo their rage. Usually they've been abandoned or excessively controlled by their mothers as much as by their fathers. Rescuers may be angry with their mothers, but their dominant motive is not to rid themselves of rage but to resurrect their fathers and show they are better women than their mothers. Rescue can also be a highly enjoyable experience for both partners, which is rarely true for Obsession. As long as it's not an extreme or destructive scenario, helping a person you love and being helped by them can be a wonderful feeling. This is what people look for in partners, and it's silly to treat this aspect of love as a pathology or an addiction.

The most extreme cases of Rescue can approach the self-destructiveness of the Obsession scenario. But Rescue comes in many forms and versions, and unlike Obsession, it often ends happily. Like the other love scenarios, it offers a chance to resolve an early trauma. The outcome largely depends on the kind of man the woman chooses to rescue, as well as her expectations about being rescued back.

Searching for the Lost Father

Mary Gordon, the novelist and essayist, has written movingly in *The Shadow Man* about how much her life was shaped by the sudden death of her beloved father when she was seven years old. For most of her young life she thought of herself as a girl whose father had died, and she has written of her mission to find and resurrect her father.

In a more recent memoir, *Seeing Through Places,* Gordon focuses more on her early relationship with her mother. After her father died, she and her newly widowed mother were forced to give up their home and move in with her grandmother, a move Gordon dreaded. In her seven-year-old mind, she wanted to stay where her beloved father had lived, in case he decided to come back. By leaving their apartment, she felt they were abandoning him. What if he came back and they weren't there? But she also knew she couldn't tell anyone what she felt, because the adults would just say that she had to accept her father's death and move on.

Children never stop praying their parent will return, and unconsciously, adults keep this hope alive as well. The death of a parent in childhood is an unacceptable loss, and many people spend their lives trying to bring their fathers or mothers back to life, if only symbolically.

To make things even harder for Gordon, after her father died, her mother drank too much and didn't cope well. She turned to her daughter to fill her needs. Emotionally, their roles were reversed, and Gordon had to be the caretaker instead of the child. She tells us that her first boyfriend was also an orphan—a young man who had recently lost both of his parents—making him even more in need of rescue than she was. But the boyfriend also came to Gordon's aid—providing a little space (literally and symbolically) from the suffocating atmosphere of life with her mother. Her mother was always too exhausted to clean the house—so every surface was covered with piles of papers and grime. Gordon's first boyfriend was the first of several who would try, in vain, to clean that house. But as Gordon recalls, no vacuum cleaner could clear that accumulation of grief.

After her first marriage failed, Gordon married an older man, someone who admired her and gave her the support she lacked as a child. Gradually she worked her way to what she wanted and needed: a man who took good care of her. But even this happy marriage didn't thoroughly quench her need to resurrect her father. When she reached middle age, she embarked on a final quest to recover her father and put him at rest.

In *The Shadow Man* Gordon describes how she set about digging through archives and traveling around the country to discover her father's true story, which had always been shrouded in mystery. She unearthed many shocking things about him, including his living family, which he had disowned as a young man—the paternal side of her family she always believed was dead. Although she couldn't bring her father back to life, she did acquire a few new relatives. And her love for him was never diminished by even the most distressing revelations of his past. But to finally accept his death, she had to take one more drastic step.

One thing she learned was how much her mother's relatives disliked her father (this made him worthy of being forgiven), and she couldn't bear to leave her father buried beside them. So in a final act of rescue and resurrection, Gordon removed her father's remains from his forty-year-old grave and reburied them in a nicer spot—a place where she and her mother and her family would join him one day.

Her quest might strike some as morbid, but Gordon was only doing (perhaps more literally) what many daughters who miss their fathers do—finding him again, or a surrogate figure, and giving him the care that her mother was not capable of providing. The wish to rescue or reunite with the lost parent is extremely common. In most cases, that effort is simply superimposed on an adult lover—which is why a rescuer refuses to give up trying to save a partner who can't or won't be saved.

Beauty and the Beast: Rescuing Yourself

People often think, wrongly, that the message of stories like *Beauty and the Beast* is that you can transform someone with your love. Love is a potent force, but you can't really change someone else; they have to change themselves, and even then only with a great deal of effort. The main point of a rescue story is not whether the wounded person has really changed from a beast to a prince (for the change is all in the eyes of the beholder). What's important is what the rescue does for the rescuer. Does it make the rescuer feel she has become a better woman than her mother? If a man is the rescuer, does he feel more manly and powerful?

Beauty fell in love with the Beast when he still looked like an animal—before he was revealed as a prince. She fell in love with him because of the qualities she saw in him: intelligence, kindness, vulnerability, and, of course, his love and need for her. She didn't try to change him, she accepted him as he was. The Beast was freed from his cursed exterior because he loved and was loved. But having him become a prince was never a condition of Beauty's love. In fact, in the first movie version of the story, Beauty does not look entirely happy with his princely transformation—she hints she will miss the Beast, and the prince must assure her that he is the same person she loved before.

Beauty and the Beast: The Hidden Story

It's worth looking closely at this story because it reveals many subtle aspects of the rescue plot. In the original folktale, Beauty lives with her father and two selfish sisters. When her father leaves for a trip, he asks his three daughters what they'd like him to bring back. Beauty's sisters ask for expensive gifts while Beauty asks only for one perfect rose. But her modest request puts her father in danger when he picks a flower from the Beast's enchanted garden.

The monster then demands the father's life—or the life of one of his daughters. By taking his place at the castle, Beauty saves her father. The Beast falls in love with her, and she grows fond of him. Out of love, he gives Beauty her freedom so that she may return to her father, who is ill and will die unless he sees that his daughter is safe. When Beauty leaves, the Beast becomes progressively weaker; he's close to death when she returns. As he dies, she declares her love, and a prince rises up from the ashes of the Beast—released from his enchantment by her love.

Two highly acclaimed films have been made of this story—the 1946 surrealistic version written and directed by the poet Jean Cocteau, and the 1991 Disney animated version. Even today, many young girls own the cartoon video and play it repeatedly.

The Disney version begins with a prologue about how the prince came to be a beast, years before he met Belle (Beauty). The young man lives in a beautiful castle and has everything, but he is selfish and spoiled. One bitterly cold night a beggar woman dressed in rags knocks on his door and offers him a magical rose in return for shelter. Repelled by her appearance, the prince orders her away, even after she warns him that looks are deceiving. Then the woman's exterior melts away to reveal a beautiful and enchanting princess. The prince begs for her forgiveness, but it's too late.

She places the prince and his domain under a curse. He is turned into a huge and ugly beast, and she gives the Beast the magic rose he had refused to accept, telling him that he can escape the curse only if he can find a woman he loves, who loves him back. But he must do this before he turns twenty-one, when he will be trapped in the curse, forever beyond redemption. The prince/Beast falls into a deep depression. He is so ashamed of his appearance that he never leaves his castle. Years pass and his time is running out.

The story now shifts to a neighboring village, where Belle lives alone with her father. Because she is beautiful, she's pursued by a macho and vain neighbor, Gaston, whom she dislikes. One day Belle's kind but bumbling father takes a trip. Missing a turn, he enters the realm of the Beast, where he's held as a prisoner until Belle takes his place.

In *Beauty and the Beast,* the heroine's mother is conveniently missing. Depending on which version of the folktale you read, Beauty either lives alone with her father or with her father and her two selfish sisters. Her love for her father is more wifely than in families where the mother is around. Psychologists usually agree that fairy tales featuring motherless heroines or evil older women or sisters are usually expressing a girl's fantasy of outdoing the other females or simply getting rid of them. The motherless heroines like Beauty have innocently replaced their mothers; these folktale heroines are also invariably more beautiful and loved than their sisters.

In the Disney version, an angry older woman sets the whole drama in motion by turning the prince into a beast and keeping him under a spell. By doing this, she also endangers the life of Belle's innocent father. The evil enchantress may be a fantasy projection of the heroine's mother; after all, a woman drawn to the rescue fantasy blames her mother for her father's problems. She also wants to prove that her goodness can reverse the damage inflicted by her mother.

After Belle moves into the enchanted castle, the Beast cleans up his appearance and learns to control his terrible temper. Belle starts to look at him differently. Although she's happy in the castle, she worries about her father. When the Beast holds up his magic mirror, a major source of his power, they see that her father is sick and may be dying. Because he loves her, the Beast tells Belle she is free to leave and may go to rescue her father. He gives her his magic mirror so she will always be able to find her way back to him.

The mirror's alternating images of the father and the Beast reveal the core meaning of Rescue stories—that the lover who needs to be rescued is actually a reflection of the woman's sick or dead father. This theme is almost always repeated in this romantic scenario.

Belle finds her father near death and revives him. But when Gaston, her rejected suitor, learns about the Beast, he calls on the townspeople to storm the castle, and sets out to kill his rival. When the castle is under siege, the Beast doesn't bother to fight back: he has become a weak and passive figure. When Belle arrives, she calls for him to fight, and the Beast is quickly roused and overcomes Gaston. But graciously, he lets his enemy go, and Gaston promptly stabs him in the back.

As the Beast is dying, he and Belle declare their love for each other, but she was too late to save him (as the daughter was in reality), and he expires. With the anguish of a child who has lost her father, she begs him not to leave her.

Suddenly the body of the dead Beast starts to rise, and his animal coat melts away. His claw becomes a hand, and we see a progressive metamorphosis—until the Beast becomes a handsome prince. He looks at Belle and says, "It's me." She looks at him and sees the gentle eyes of the Beast. She agrees, "It is you." In the end, they live happily together with her father in the beautiful castle.

The connection in this story between lover and father who both need rescuing could not be more obvious. But the story calls attention to two other central features of the Rescue scenario that require explanation: the missing or destructive mother and the fierce and carnal creature who becomes passive until Beauty rouses him to action. These two themes are inseparable from the primary plot of resurrecting a lost father. They turn up regularly in Rescue plots, in real life and fiction.

The Rescuer Lets Her Mother Die

The unconscious fantasy of outdoing a mother who was not loving enough is a typical feature of Rescue plots. These children blame their mothers for the loss of their fathers, and also resent having to become surrogate partners at a time in life when they need to be cared for themselves. But very few women who are rescuers set out to destroy or replace their mothers, at least not consciously. In many fairy tales of rescue, the mother (instead of the father) just happens to be dead. Maybe the daughter who has lost her beloved father unconsciously feels she lost the wrong parent. In the fairy tale, her anger is expressed by switching the positions of who is dead and who is alive. Of course, even women who are angry or disappointed about their mothers' faults almost always feel great love and attachment for their mother. But in some insightful Rescue movies, the mother's destructiveness is openly portrayed, and the heroine might even have to let her mother die either to be happy herself or to clear the way for the rescues of her father, her lover, and herself.

The mutual hatred between mother and daughter is the theme of the 1942 Bette Davis classic, *Now, Voyager.* Charlotte Vale is the youngest and unwanted daughter of a widowed Boston dowager.

Charlotte's father died when she was a young child, and her mother raised her to be a spinster and companion in her old age. When Charlotte was young and pretty, her mother destroyed her relationships with boys, and eventually Charlotte capitulated to the role of old maid, becoming stout, unattractive, and withdrawn. She looks her mother's age and hides in her room, silently carving wooden boxes.

As the movie opens, Charlotte is on the verge of a "nervous breakdown," and her sister-in-law has called on the psychiatrist Dr. Jaquith (Claude Rains) to save her. The doctor immediately sees the mother's destructiveness and takes Charlotte with him to his country rest home. In just weeks, the awkward ugly duckling begins to turn into a beautiful woman. It starts with her doctor removing her glasses (she doesn't need these anymore, Jaquith tells her). He has always seen the attractive woman hidden beneath the dowdy exterior. To help her to separate from her mother and complete the metamorphosis, he prescribes a long ocean voyage.

On the ship, Charlotte meets a handsome, married architect (Paul Henreid). They have an affair, and Charlotte begins to see herself as a desirable woman. He's separated from his wife, but he can't divorce her because he wants to care for his emotionally disturbed little girl, who is unloved by her mother.

Back at home, Charlotte no longer takes orders from her mother. She meets and becomes engaged to a handsome and rich widower, a Boston Brahmin. But just before the wedding, her shipboard lover shows up and Charlotte breaks off the engagement. This rebellion so infuriates her mother (who was pleased that her family was joining with the widower's even more distinguished one) that she has a heart attack and dies.

Feeling that she caused her mother's death, Charlotte returns to Dr. Jaquith's rest home. Here she meets the architect's daughter and discovers that they have much in common. She takes care of the child and pulls her out of her depression. So having been saved by Dr. Jaquith and her architect lover, Charlotte in turn rescues the child. Charlotte must choose between continuing her affair with the child's father or becoming a surrogate mother for his child. She chooses the child.

Many interpreters of this film have seen this choice as an act of self-sacrifice, but it's clear that Charlotte has recognized her lover's limitations and sees greater value and happiness in choosing the child. Moreover, her status at the clinic is now elevated to colleague and benefactor to the handsome Dr. Jaquith, her original rescuer. The movie can't quite show her marrying her psychiatrist (although in 1940 this was less taboo than divorce). But it ends with the suggestion that Charlotte has become more of a partner than a patient to her former savior; we see them sitting by a cozy fire in the beautiful house that now belongs to her, going over Charlotte's plans to add a wing to Jaquith's hospital with the wealth that she inherited from her mother.

"Is this the same woman I first met here?" Jaquith asks the now beautiful Charlotte—the same incredulous question Beauty had put to the Beast. Of course she is the same woman, and he can see it, gazing deeply into her eyes, which are no longer covered by heavy brows and glasses. This movie is famous for its line: "Why ask for the moon when you can have the stars?" That is her answer to the architect when he feels she is sacrificing too much for him. But in fact Charlotte does get it all in the end—her mother's money, the best man of the three in her life, and a stepdaughter (her younger self) who is now in the loving care of Jaquith and herself.

Now, Voyager is about a woman who is rescued by two men and in turn rescues a child. She shares the history of paternal loss (and being used by her mother as a substitute husband) with many other daughters who rescue men. But in this version of the story, her anger with her mother—and her willingness to kill her mother so that she might live—are more openly expressed. The rescuer's ultimate goal is to be rescued by a man who will give her the care and protection she never got from her father. And that goal is also more directly expressed in

Now, Voyager. Instead of saving a man so that he may save her back, Charlotte takes a more direct route to being saved and winds up with a strong man and an innocent child she may save in return.

First her psychiatrist rescues Charlotte from her destructive mother, then an attractive lover validates her identity as a sexually desirable woman. Being loved by these two men allows her to love and nurture a child who is suffering as she once did. She triumphs over her mother by reclaiming her sexuality and showing that she is a better parent.

The Tamed Beast

The anger toward the mother, which is disguised in *Beauty and the Beast*, is treated openly in *Now, Voyager.* But there is one more hidden theme in *Beauty and the Beast* that needs examining, because it explains a key feature of the Rescue plot. It concerns male aggression, and how the heroine deals with it.

A beast is a carnal figure, and he's supposed to be fierce. But before Belle can love him, he has to become a more gentle figure (learn to control his temper in the Disney version). In both the Disney and Cocteau film versions of the story, the Beast has even become too passive to fight for his life. In the Cocteau version, when Beauty implores him to live, he answers that if he were a man he might fight, but beasts can only grovel on the ground and die.

In every version of this tale, the Beast is ready to give up and die until Beauty convinces him that she loves and needs him. Her love releases him from his passivity as well as from his curse. In other words, Beauty takes control of the Beast's aggression. He is gentle and kind until she tells him to fight—then he rears up and growls when she calls on him to assert his carnal nature.

This suggests that Beauty is divided about whether she wants a tame or aggressive beast. She clearly wants both, but she also wants to be in control of his aggresion.

No heroine wants a lover who can't fight for himself, but for women who are frightened by male aggression, there's a definite appeal to a lover who will rise up or lie down upon her command— a lover whose aggression is subject to her control.

Some women's wounded fathers could also be frightening. Perhaps they were alcoholics who became frightening when drunk, or they lost their tempers and hit their wives. A daughter of such a situation would be reassured if she had some control over her wounded lover's aggression.

Not all women rescuers had aggressive fathers, but in picking men to save, they are frequently drawn to men who are depressed. These women don't want a passive man, but they do need to feel in control, given all the loss they have suffered. They want a man they feel will never leave them, which often means a man who is dependent on them. This eliminates a lot of anxiety for women who lost their father in childhood.

Another kind of woman who is often drawn to dependent men is the one who had an all-powerful father who dominated the household and made everyone bend to his will. These fathers may be frightening because their daughters can never meet their high expectations. This daughter needs a partner who will appreciate and admire her and will let her be the center of attention, as she never was as a child. But her partner's passivity may bother her because she doesn't see this trait sometimes comes with the others she requires.

Daughters of Titans

Kelly Donovan was terrified of her father, although everyone else admired and adored him. He'd overcome great adversity and had become an outstanding athlete. He'd fought in Vietnam and won a medal for physical bravery. He was competent at everything—intellectually and physically. He took care of all of his poor relatives and neighbors who needed help. He established a foundation to bring meals to the sick and the old. Everyone who knew him looked up to him as a god. But as a child Kelly found him terrifying because nothing she did was ever impressive enough. He barely noticed her, and around him, she felt very timid.

Kelly was drawn to men who were nothing like her father. She married a garden designer who was sensitive and kind and who let Kelly's work as a real estate agent come first. Kelly loved her husband Rich's gentle nature, but she wished he would earn more money. Instead of appreciating the care and support and freedom he gave her, Kelly spent too much time nagging Rich and trying to change him. She couldn't see she chose Rich because she needed a man who would admire her and let her be in charge.

Kelly did not have a wounded or missing father, but she didn't have a father who noticed and admired her. She didn't need to recover a lost father, but she needed admiration. Because Rich was not as financially successful as her father, she just couldn't see that she had gotten what she had wanted.

Kelly's marriage had many gratifying elements. She and Rich shared most interests, and he was a terrific father to their three children. He was much less critical of them than Kelly could be and wonderfully playful. In that way, Kelly was able to give her children the father that she never had. When she paid the bills, she believed she was taking care of him, but Rich rescued her just as much, by being a husband who supported the success of everyone else in the family. This rescue relationship would be mutually gratifying, if only Kelly didn't expect a man who combined Rich's supportiveness with the ambition and drive of her father.

Women who marry losers—men who won't stop drinking or exploiting their partners—are living out an entirely different Rescue story. These are the relationships that give Rescue a bad reputation, because the women get nothing in return for all they give.

Damaged Beyond Redemption

Among the most extreme cases are women who fall in love with violent men—even criminals who are locked behind bars. These women are determined to see a wounded prince in someone everyone else sees as a monster.

It's surprising how many convicted serial rapists and murderers—men who will be locked up for twenty years to life—find women who love them, write to them, and visit them for years, and who even marry them in telephone ceremonies. What could these women see in these men? Many of these rescuing angels probably don't want to be in a real relationship. For them, saving a man who is safely locked away becomes a substitute for genuine intimacy. Thinking you can rehabilitate a murderer or a rapist is the ultimate challenge in Rescue, and some of these women are attracted to their extreme masculine aggression—as long as the men are kept behind steel bars. They have their tamed beasts. One wonders what would happen to these relationships if the men were ever released.

A March 25, 1999, article in the *New York Times* discussed the growing popularity of these relationships, facilitated by E-mail. The article features Diane, a psychotherapist (of all things) from Colorado who was engaged to a man who had spent six years on death row for killing another prisoner in a fight. Her fiancé had been in prison for twenty years, and they plan to marry when he is released—in the next year or two. Diane didn't want her last name used, because "my parents don't know that I've fallen in love with someone in prison."

One might think a therapist would be the last person to fall in love with a death row prisoner. But many therapists have particularly strong Rescue orientations. (Which is fortunate, since they are willing to wait for years to see their patients get better.) Some are not able to keep the Rescue impulse in check and choose partners they would warn their patients against. Many female criminal defense attorneys are also rescuers—and are prone to getting emotionally involved with their most dangerous clients. These women often rationalize their involvement by seeing these men as victims of their childhood or the legal system rather than as aggressors. A female judge (who had once been a criminal defense attorney) also told me she believed some female defense lawyers are attracted to their violent clients for the same reason as the prison pen pals: the men represent an animal-like male sexuality that is safely locked up.

In *The Crime of Sheila McGough,* Janet Malcolm reports the true story of an innocent criminal attorney who wound up in prison because she refused to save herself if it would hurt the con man she was defending, a man who had badly used her. The prosecutor who argued she was implicated in her client's fraudulent deals implied a motive of love, although Malcolm is convinced they weren't having sex. Whether or not there was any romance, Sheila McGough as a lawyer displayed many traits of women who act out bad Rescue love stories. As Malcolm observes, when she failed to defend her con man successfully, she would not accept the guilty verdict. Instead she kept appealing when anyone else would have given up. She refused to "close the book" on his case. McGough had no sense of limits—of when to stop pouring her energy into a lost and undeserving cause. As Malcolm concludes, although she knew how to "play the violin" to save her clients, she'd never do anything like that to save herself. McGough had to sacrifice herself in order to see herself as good.

But criminal courts and prisons are not the only places where extreme cases of Rescue are found. Far more common are the millions of ordinary women who stay married to alcoholics or drug abusers who are violent, sadistic, and exploitative. Not all of these wives were consciously looking for losers, but they have a great deal of trouble leaving because they see their husbands as wounded victims. Some of these women married young and were simply naive. But either way, when a woman denies what everyone can see—that her abusive, loser partner will never change—she is trapped in a Rescue scenario that can only bring misery.

Tina Turner's Story

One well-known story of how Rescue can become self-destructive is that of rock star Tina Turner, told in her memoir *I, Tina,* and the autobiographical film *What's Love Got to Do with It?* When Anna Mae Bullock (Tina) first met Ike in 1958, she was young and naive. Like many rescuers, she had grown up without a father (her mother wouldn't even discuss him). According to Tina, her mother was no help; her behavior toward Tina ranged from neglect to exploitation.

When they first met, Ike already had a musical band and a chorus of adoring women. To the young Tina, Ike was a hero and a god. He was struck by the power of her voice and her stage presence, and he said he would turn her into a star. Their relationship started out as a Pygmalion story but it soon changed into a Rescue story (as they frequently do)—with Tina taking care of her wounded mentor. From the start, Ike made Tina promise she would never leave him, as all the other women in his life had. Most mentors in Pygmalion relationships fear they'll be deserted once their protégée graduates. But Ike's fear of being left resonated with Tina's history of early losses—and she vowed never to leave him.

Tina's fame grew and her success soon outdistanced Ike's. The higher she rose, the more he resented her talent and celebrity. Soon he became brutally violent—punching, choking, raping, and regularly beating her to a pulp. He also exploited her professionally and humiliated her with his open infidelity.

But despite his cruelty, Tina always rationalized Ike's behavior because she couldn't bear the thought of giving up on him and hurting him by leaving. She found it easier to feel his pain than to feel her own. This is common among rescuers: focusing on the other person's vulnerability lets them feel more control. It took Tina twenty years to realize she didn't need Ike. After she left him, she went on to even greater success.

Tina's story illustrates an important point about love and self-esteem. A person may be remarkably self-confident in some areas of their lives and still feel totally undeserving when it comes to love. As a singer, Tina was always a powerful and uninhibited performer, even before huge crowds, but in relation to Ike, she felt frightened and worthless. People in unhappy relationships don't necessarily have pervasive low self-esteem. Their problem with feeling undeserving is very specific to love.

The hero of the movie *Mona Lisa* is also blind to the truth about the woman he loves. George (Bob Hoskins) has just been released from prison and finds a job as a chauffeur and protector to Simone (Cathy Tyson), a high-priced prostitute. He falls in love with her, and becoming her savior gives him a much-needed purpose. Ultimately, he risks his life to help Simone find someone *she* wants to save. George is driven so strongly by his Rescue impulses that he doesn't see Simone clearly at all. He can't see that she'll never love him and that to her, he was "nothing more than a butler."

Both George and Tina Turner share a problem that is common to rescuers. They focus more easily on their partner's feelings and needs than on their own. They would sooner die than stop helping their partners—in these two cases, people who don't even care about them. Helping someone else makes them feel less vulnerable.

What Is Loving "Too Much"?

How do we know when we are loving "too much"—when we're wasting our efforts on someone who can't or won't be helped, some-one who will never bring us happiness? Some insight is provided by the recent Robin Williams film, *What Dreams May Come.*

In this story, Chris (a pediatrician played by Robin Williams) and Annie (an artist) are happily married soul mates. They have a good life until their two children are killed in a car accident. Chris recovers, but Annie sinks into a suicidal depression and is hospitalized. After it seems that she's chosen not to heal, Chris tells her that he is choosing to live and wants her to come home to him. But if she chooses death and despair over life, he wants a divorce. By giving this ultimatum, Chris rescues her, and she recovers.

Soon after, Chris is killed in an auto accident when he tries to save another victim. He goes to heaven, and being open to joy, finds that life there can have its pleasures—including being reunited with his children. The one thing he misses is Annie—and then he learns that she will never join them because she committed a sin that has sent her to hell. After losing Chris, she killed herself.

In this Rescue movie, having faith allows you to have a joyful life both on earth and in heaven. But the person in despair—the person who has lost hope—is portrayed as making a hell out of life as well as being condemned to eternal damnation. Chris wants to do what no one else has done before—enter hell and find Annie and lead her away. But all his guides warn him that he'll never find his way back. This had been his own assumption, the first time he had saved her after their children died.

Now Chris reevaluates what he did back then. He decides that in life, when he refused to join Annie in her despair, he was really pushing away his own pain so that he wouldn't drown in it. And by refusing to be drawn into her pain, he had separated from Annie. This time, he'll forgo the joy that awaits him in heaven to be with her in hell.

This turns out to be the degree of love required to save her. His refusal to give up the effort to save her, despite dire warnings from others, allows him to rescue her the second time—this time more nobly, because he is willing to share fully in her pain.

That is the movie's message, and it is very romantic. It tells viewers that really loving someone means being prepared to lose themselves in their partner's world of pain. But that message is totally wrong. Chris was actually right the first time, and not the second. We can try to save someone by saying, come with me and choose life. But if they won't choose life, we ultimately lose our own lives if we remain attached to them.

The difference between Chris's first and second approach shows the distinction between Rescue scenarios that hold promise and those that are hopeless. Many rescuers choose partners who are very disturbed or problematic, and are not willing or able to change. These rescuers keep telling themselves they can make the relationship work. They remain unrealistically optimistic in the face of their partner's unending depression or repeated betrayals. More realistically, they should give up that kind of relationship, unless the partner shows definite evidence of progress. Truthfully, we can never make someone else change.

But naturally, the rescuer hates to give up because she's already had so many losses, and she wants to believe she can still save her father and be more successful than her mother. But a lot of what happens in the relationship is not in her control—any more than it was in the original loss.

When Men Rescue Women

Men engage in Rescue scenarios as often as women do. Though their stories have much in common, in some ways they are different. Men who fall in love with women they want to rescue are also, unconsciously, repeating a childhood drama. Symbolically, they are rescuing their mothers—a responsibility that fell to them early because their fathers were missing or deficient. Often their mothers were sick or depressed, and they had to provide her with support she wasn't getting from her husband or another adult.

Their first experience of caring for a woman, their mother, made them frightened of women. To a boy a woman's needs or demands are overwhelming. Thereafter, they tend to find women too threatening. They feel more comfortable with a woman who is weak or wounded and in need of rescue. This allows them to reenact their original relationship, except this time they're in a stronger position. They can feel more like a potent man than an overwhelmed child.

In the same way that some female rescuers need a man who is relatively passive, male rescuers feel more comfortable with a woman who is ill or dependent on them. Demands from strong women make male rescuers feel impotent or castrated. A woman who is "fallen," weak, or dependent is less frightening. A woman who needs him to rescue her makes him feel less anxious and therefore more easily aroused. With a wounded woman, he doesn't have to worry about being castrated or criticized.

When Mother Needs Him

Sal Torre was sixteen years old when his mother developed breast cancer. Within weeks of his mother's diagnosis, his father had moved in with another woman, leaving Sal to be his mother's main emotional support, taking his father's place.

His mother was lucky—her treatment was successful and her cancer has not returned. But twenty years later Sal, at thirty-six, is still taking care of her. She still claims to be dying, though everyone else can see that she is as strong as a horse. Sal has never married, because he feels too guilty and frightened. He's afraid if he marries, his mother would die, and it would be his fault. And he is so attached to his mother that the thought of her dying terrifies him. His worry that she will die also suggests an unconscious wish that he be set free. That's partly why he feels so terrified and guilty.

The women he has dated were all needy and sick. They are the only ones who don't frighten him and the only ones who make him feel potent. He's never been attracted to a strong woman. But he also breaks up with the needy women he dates because he easily finds fault with them.

Sal's story is mirrored by several movies about middle-aged bachelors still living with their widowed mothers. The classic film *Marty* (starring Ernest Borgnine, which was based on a play starring Rod Steiger) is about a middle-aged son who falls in love for the first time. He's drawn to a girl his friends describe as a "dog." She had almost given up hope of marrying, as Marty had, so when they find each other, it's a mutual rescue. But Marty must overcome his mother's resistance and his guilt over leaving her.

A modern version of the *Marty* story, called *Only the Lonely*, featured John Candy as a policeman and Maureen O'Hara as his widowed mother, who was a force to be reckoned with. He falls in love (with Ally Sheedy), but any intimacy with his girlfriend is always disrupted by his mother's intrusions, including his own fantasies that his mother is dying. Of course, his mother is a tower of strength, and when her son finally leaves, she is quite able to take care of herself.

Men Who Classify Women As Madonnas or Whores

When Brent Donavan was young he was always attracted to women his peers called "ho's" or "whores"—slutty women. He recalls, "I saw something in them that they didn't see in themselves—an untouched potential that I could help them fulfill."

In addition to these girls not being the kind he could bring home to his family, he was never successful in his pursuit of them. "These kinds of women are attracted to bad guys. They didn't think they deserved to be treated well, or else they saw my motives—that I was interested in more than treating them badly. They weren't ready for that, or didn't think they deserved it."

Brent may be correct that some of these women weren't ready for a man who would treat them well, but it's also possible that they didn't see themselves as "fallen" and in need of saving. He didn't recognize his own motives and needs in his attraction to these women he thought of as slutty. Instead he blamed their disinterest on what he saw as low self-esteem. In fact, many objects of rehabilitation are unwilling partners in the Rescue drama. They don't think there's anything wrong with them. In the movie *Chasing Amy*, the narrator loses the girl he loves because he wants to erase a past that she's not ashamed of. Even people with real problems—like alcoholics—usually don't view their situation the same way their rescuer does.

Brent explains his attraction to "ho's" as a passing stage of adolescence. Now he is happily married to a "healthy" and "well-adjusted" wife and talks about romantic love as though it's just manufactured by the movies. Marriage is not about passion or romance, he proclaims. But one wonders whether he splits women into two categories—fallen women who are sexually attractive and women who make good wives but are more like friends and working partners than objects of passion. Brent's rescue inclinations are not particularly extreme, but his family history is consistent with putting women into separate sexual and marital partner categories.

Brent was closer to his mother and thought his father was less patient with her than he might have been. Brent and his mother are social while his father was more of an introvert, he says. While he certainly wasn't forced into a *Marty* role, Brent probably had to provide some of the attention his mother didn't get from her husband.

Loving the Woman Who Is Ill

Sharon Teller was surprised, at the age of sixty, when she suddenly found a boyfriend (after years of being unattached) within weeks of suffering a heart attack. Given her long history of being on her own, and the scarcity of men who are interested in older women, she thought her love life might be over. She certainly didn't expect her illness to add to her sexual appeal.

When an old acquaintance suddenly announced his sexual interest in her, and they started an affair, Sharon wondered why her love life had taken this unexpected turn. Was she becoming more tolerant and open to a relationship, now that she felt more vulnerable and afraid of being sick and alone? This was possible, she thought, but her behavior hadn't really undergone any dramatic transformation.

It slowly dawned on Sharon that sickness actually attracts a certain kind of man—a man who feels more potent with a woman who is vulnerable. As Sharon grew stronger over the next few months, her partner's sexual interest waned.

This turns out to be a common problem when men are drawn to vulnerable women: they may not really want the woman to get better, and if she does, they have difficulty becoming sexually aroused.

Of course, not all male rescuers need to keep their partners sick. In the movie *Now, Voyager,* Dr. Jaquith wanted Charlotte to get better. He was a strong man who wasn't threatened by his equal—but technically he was her psychiatrist, and not her lover. In *What Dreams May Come*, the hero initially fell in love with the heroine because she was strong and his match—she collapsed only after losing her family—so he wasn't turned on by weakness.

But when women are chosen specifically to be rescued, their lovers often find them less sexually appealing as they gain strength because this arouses an anxiety from their childhood of being overpowered. In contrast, most women rescuers want their men to shape up because this would prove they are better than their mothers.

When self-help books argue that rescuers are making self-destructive choices that will make them unhappy, they miss the main consideration. The issue is not necessarily whether the partner really changes—but rather what that partner does for the rescuer. Does the love object make the man feel stronger? Does he make the woman feel she is more loving than her mother? Rescuers may see qualities that no one else sees in their partners. But as long as their partners make them feel better rather than worse about themselves—and this effect can be sustained over time—the relationship can be a gratifying one.

Rescuing Someone Who Wont Live Long

Another variation of this romantic scenario involves people who fall in love with partners who are doomed to die soon. In some situations, like old age, the proximity of death might be a given rather than a choice. But for people who are able to fall in love only with a dying partner, it's a different story.

Strange as it sounds, some people who have trouble making a commitment find it easier to throw themselves into an intense relationship with someone who won't be around for more than a year. Think of Romeo and Juliet, heading for death from the moment they fall in love.

In one classic rescue film, *Dark Victory,* Bette Davis plays a socialite who is dying of a brain tumor and has less than a year to live. Her surgeon, who had always been a bachelor married only to his work, falls in love for the first time with this patient, and marries her even though he knows she is doomed to die in a matter of months.

She's a safe choice because she's ill and he won't have to face a long commitment. In this union, there isn't any possibility of having children—so he doesn't have to become a father. Even after their wedding he's really still more wedded to his research—although his work obsession is rationalized because he's trying to find the cure for brain cancer (and oddly enough, this 1939 fictional surgeon was sixty years ahead of his time by proposing something close to the modern concept of angiogenesis). The movie ends with Bette Davis dying bravely and alone, having sent her husband off to a medical conference, even though she's felt the symptoms that tell her she will die within hours. The surgeon is obviously so wrapped up in his work he doesn't even notice that Bette Davis has lost her vision, the sign that death is near.

In some ways, this love story illustrates the problem of fearing commitment, the subject of the next chapter. A man who fears getting trapped in marriage will have an easier time entering one that can't last a year. But this is a Rescue story too. Being a brain surgeon, this character has shown he's a rescuer at heart, one who is willing to take up lost causes. Picking a woman who is doomed relieves the guilt many rescuers feel. It won't be his fault when Bette Davis dies. She was doomed before he met her, and he's giving her the chance to have a happy life before she dies. Unlike Marty or John Candy in *Only the Lonely* he doesn't have to grapple with guilt. This surgeon is not alone. For some rescuers, illness is intertwined with love.

A Life of Rescue: Molly

At different points in our lives most of us experience Rescue, and we usually get to try each role (the rescuer, the one saved). The ultimate goal of the rescuer is to be saved herself, so it's logical that most people will alternate parts. Molly has lived many different versions of the story—all highly dramatic and extreme. She is thirty-six years old and has never been married, although she's had three long relationships and is currently involved in a promising one. Molly lives near Seattle and is a high school biology teacher. She is also a serious student of Buddhism. Her childhood background is classic for women who act out extreme or repeated versions of Rescue.

"My father was an alcoholic, he would get rageful when he was drunk. He'd beat my mother, my brother, and to some extent—me. The aggression went down the line—I felt the repercussions of his violence—when he beat my brother, my brother was violent to me.

"My father [a physician] beat my mother pretty regularly, but I don't have a good memory of it—there are a lot of holes in my memory. Sometimes he was just violent with objects. He'd take food out of the refrigerator and throw it on the kitchen wall. He'd throw the stereo on the floor and jump up and down on it. When I was in the room he was less directly physical with my mother. But if I was upstairs it was worse. He'd throw my mother down the stairs. I'm not sure how long this went on. Part of me thinks it was my whole childhood. Sometimes I think there were some happy years—I haven't been able to get a clear idea from my family.

"My father was very controlling. I was definitely the one who was closest to him, of all the kids. When I was younger I probably knew him better than anybody, and he would talk to me about stuff, but he's fairly arrogant and it keeps him from letting people see him. He uses it as a shield. My parents didn't divorce until I was in the seventh grade, and I was definitely the kid in the family who was sitting on the fence. I was close to Mom, but I was trying hard to love Dad too. When my brother outright rejected him, and he was made out to be the monster, I said he's not a monster. Some of the things he's doing are monsterlike, but he's not a monster.

"I remember as a little kid sitting with him at the kitchen table and he was crying, the morning after he'd been violent and he'd been unable to control himself. I'm not justifying it, but he couldn't control his rage—it was probably something chemical in his body. Then he'd come around, and it would move me. I took on the battered-wife syndrome as a kid. I always said if we just love him more he won't hit us. It always meant a lot to him that I didn't jump on the bandwagon and say you are just a flaming asshole."

Although Molly is half-joking in saying she took on the "battered-wife syndrome as a child," she knows it is really true. She wasn't sexually abused by her father, but since childhood, she felt she was the family member closest to him. As far back as childhood she saw herself as his true partner, even more than her mother, and from the start she rationalized his dreadful behavior. Decades later, she is the only one in the family who has a relationship with her father. She's deeply attached to him and still trying really hard to work things out. Most female rescuers have also had problematic relationships with their mothers—generally their mothers were difficult or needy, and Molly's mother was no exception.

In the minds of many female rescuers, the father is unconsciously mixed up with a lover—and not only in adulthood, when she reenacts the story. The confusion goes back to adolescence, or earlier, when she stepped into her mother's shoes.

In the movie *Eve's Bayou,* the physician-father (Samuel Jackson) is a sexual philanderer who fails to come home night after night. His oldest daughter Cicely (his favorite child) is just reaching adolescence, and starts to blame her mother for her father's absence. As her mother begins to fight with her father, Cicely's relationship with her father takes on more erotic overtones. She's the one who always defends him and waits up for him until he comes home. One night, after hearing her parents arguing and her father collapsing in the living room, Cicely approaches him from the back, massaging his shoulders, and offering the comfort she thinks her mother is withholding. That gesture suddenly turns into something more explicitly sexual.

Like Molly and her mother, the rescuing daughter in *Eve's Bayou* also has a very hazy memory, full of holes, of exactly what happened that night. This is certainly true of Molly's description of her child-hood—so vivid in some ways, so vague in others. And according to Molly, her mother, also, was always lost in a fog.

"There have been long periods when my mother just isn't in touch with herself—a lot of disconnect. I've heard she was a gifted artist, but I've never seen any of her paintings. Early on, something happened in their marriage. The paintings and art materials were discarded and it's a form of control by my father in his bizarre, awful way—he was taking things away from her that she loved, that made her who she was.

"I think things took a turn for the worse when I was in the third grade, but my mother feels my father acted out even before I was conceived. I don't want to delve into it with my mother because she's stuck in the past already. They separated several times when I was in elementary school and got divorced when I was in the seventh grade."

Molly was naturally frightened of men when she was young. It was hard for her to move out of her mother's house, and she attended junior college because she wasn't ready to leave. Her mother also desperately relied on her. In Molly's view, her mother was always lost in a haze of alcohol and drugs, partly because of the abuse she suffered. She also hurt her back and started taking painkillers and drinking in order to feel better.

It took Molly a long time before she trusted any boy enough to have sex with him. She dated her first boyfriend, Lou, for ten months before they had sex. In fact, she decided he was trustworthy only after he rescued her from her own mother. It was her birthday, during the summer after her freshman year of college, and the first time she'd invited a boyfriend to her home. They found her mother upstairs, in bed, totally smashed.

"Lou showed up [for the birthday celebration] and he didn't bat an eye and he handled the situation so well. He didn't shame my mother. He talked to her as an adult. I tried not to wake her up. She came down drunk and angry that she hadn't been included. And he said, 'Sober up and you'll be included.' He didn't reject me because of her. He didn't say 'you're a drunken slob.' He said, 'Wow, this is painful, this is Molly's birthday, what are you doing?' He just pointed out the obvious. We were all in tears, and Lou was talking to my mother. He was so human, something shifted in our relationship— for the first time, I totally trusted him. He was a totally trustworthy guy. But he was somewhat uncomplicated. He didn't have the character of a poet that I'm drawn to in men. He was so direct and uncomplicated he was almost boring."

She stayed with Lou in a pleasant but noncommitted relationship for six years. She felt that although he was nice to her, he often seemed to drift off, to not be present. Then Molly came down with encephalitis and nearly died, and it totally changed her life. She feels that going through this experience instigated a larger healing process. While she was sick, Lou took care of her, and when she recovered, she went to India for six months to pursue spiritual learning. When Lou told her he wanted to come, she assumed he would propose and they would marry. But when he arrived in India, their relationship became uncomfortable, and it began to end. She stayed in India for ten months and then on and off for two years.

When she came back finally, she told Lou she either wanted them to be together or she was moving across the country to live in the center run by her spiritual teacher; that would be her family if he couldn't commit himself. Lou was frightened by the pressure and said he didn't want to be the reason she stayed. Only later did she learn how hard it had been for him when she went to India, and how much he had worried when her letters from India didn't reach him.

Her next serious boyfriend, Richard, was eighteen years older than Molly—she was twenty-eight and he was forty-six or forty-seven when they met. He'd been married twice before, had a son Molly's age, and wanted to marry her. Molly knew she didn't want Richard for a life partner. But she didn't want to break up with him because she liked being with someone who wanted to marry her, even though she thought they would not wind up together.

Then Richard was diagnosed with cancer and died just six months later. In her spiritual manner, Molly feels that they were both right about their relationship. Richard wanted to spend the rest of his life with her (which he did), and the relationship didn't last—as Molly had expected.

When Richard was dying, he opened up to her completely, and Molly feels honored that he put his life in her hands. "He just trusted me to be the best I could be and that I could do the best for him." To her, it was a beautiful experience, even though it was sad.

When he was diagnosed with cancer, Richard was living about a hundred miles from where Molly lived. He was surrounded by friends and was deeply involved in his community. When he realized he was dying, he told Molly he wanted to move in with her and live with her for the rest of his life. She worried about handling the stress, and it made her nervous he'd be leaving all his friends to live with her. She was filled with conflict.

"I didn't know if I could do this. I'd done a lot of caretaking of my mother—she was disabled all her life because of my father's violence. It may have been irrational, but I thought I would get sick if he came to live with me—that the effects of my encephalitis would come back. I had only so much juice. He felt he couldn't do the spiritual changes he needed to do in his old environment—he could only do it with me. I felt I couldn't do it alone. I felt I was being sucked into a black hole.

"Then a friend who was also studying with my spiritual teacher said she could see that Richard was clear about what he needed, and he was the one who was dying. She thought he needed to be with me, not with his friends. She said, 'Molly, when the shit hits the fan and you can't handle his physical demands I'll relieve you. I'll come and live with you and help you—even if it takes six months.'

"I knew Richard would become paralyzed—we'd been told that. I knew he'd need total care, but I also didn't know if we were talking about six years or two months. After being treated for five months with radiation, Richard moved up here, and we rented a house on the ocean for a month. He ended up dying in that summer rental, after just a month. Almost right after he came he was bedridden, and I called up my friend and said, 'Come.' She came to be with us for as long as it would take. I needed someone standing on the living side of things or I would have gone with him.

"When he asked to live with me, I was struggling with the decision. I have a disabled parent, and I have given a lot of care. But I didn't think I could do this alone. With my friend's help I could go into this unknown place and go with it, fearlessly. There was someone who would pull me out. It's not just that I was afraid of death. Richard was my partner—I was losing him, I was going through this major loss too. It was pretty dramatic.

"It ended up that once he was sick, he went quickly. He was in a coma for ten days. So it only impacted my friend's life for two weeks, but she is so bighearted. We are both practicing Buddhists—it's important to help people die. It's a serious honor to help—not that many people will ask you. My friend appeased my fear enough to let me be big. I can't be that big alone."

After Richard died, Molly wasn't involved with anyone for a long time. She's now in a relationship with a man named Terry who is very caring. In the past year, Molly has been in two serious car accidents. The first one shattered one of her legs and the second one badly injured her shoulder. She's had to have several operations, and Terry, who'd initially acted tuned out or remote (like her first boyfriend) has become more committed and attentive to her, now that she's really dependent. Molly's first boyfriend was also devoted to her when she was sick, but aside from his kindness and sensitivity, there wasn't a lot to hold them together.

Molly isn't the least bit bored by Terry. Like her other boyfriends, he plays the costarring role in her primary drama of Rescue, but Molly is attracted to a lot of his qualities, and they share many interests and values. It seems she has finally found somebody who will make her Rescue fantasy turn out happily, and he has other good qualities as well. This is essential to a satisfying relationship.

A relationship built on just one note—one's formative problem—is unlikely to work and usually ends by confirming your worst fears instead of resolving them. If you pick someone only because they allow you to reenact your trauma, it suggests your need is extreme. In that case, unconsciously you've probably picked someone who will only increase your anxiety instead of reducing it, and you'll have no other shared interests that are necessary for building a satisfying relationship. There seems to be an optimal degree of resonance that your partner should have with your love scenario: not too much, not too little, and not the only thing that attracts you.

Molly has matured enough to look more objectively at a lover and to ask the hard question that needs to be asked—will this person make me happy? Because Terry has become more committed to her since her leg and shoulder were injured, they must have reciprocal

Rescue needs that are met in this relationship, in addition to many other points of attraction. Of course, it concerns Molly that her injuries seemed to have had a beneficial effect on her relationship. She wonders if sickness must always play a role in any relationship she has—which is a very good question indeed. But now that Molly is getting what she needs, and Terry has been acting in a way that reassures her, she is probably just more perceptive and reflective about her romantic life than most.

"One thing I haven't had the guts to explore with myself is the intertwining of medical problems and codependence. I was with someone who got sick and depended on me, and in my first relationship I had encephalitis and that boyfriend took care of me. In my third relationship I've had all these injuries and problems with walking, and my partner is taking care of me. I don't think it's really true, but part of me is scared that there's a reason I get sick—so nobody will leave anyone else.

"I felt manipulated by my mother's illness. I had a hard time leaving her when I went to college—that's why I went to a college just a half hour away. I felt so worried about her, and she was trashed and I felt I needed to take care of her. So it's weird that there is always some kind of dependency involved in deep love for me. In all three of my relationships a medical problem kept the relationship going. You'd think it would make the relationship fall apart, but it held it together. [She also notes that her father is a doctor and is uneasy about what this might mean.]

"When I had encephalitis it stressed my relationship, but my partner didn't leave me when I was sick. But after I got healthy, I left him. If a medical problem arises, I get confused, and I go to places other people might not emotionally.

"If I am sick, I can put myself first. All I know is that physical problems were a huge thing in my mother's life and mine, and my brother has also had problems. I'm more likely to choose to help than to die myself. I don't have a weird fascination with bad health, but my father, who is a doctor, didn't see my experience with Richard's death as a beautiful thing. He said 'You've had so much to deal with, why don't you stay away from crises for a while?'

"For a while, it scared me and made me think, oh my God, am I addicted to crises? There's possibly some truth to both our views. He can't deal with me being in pain, so he'd rather have me live a suburban life and watch television than have a deeply emotional and spiritual life that might involve helping a friend die. But he can't handle that kind of intimacy and emotional exchange himself, so he can't see me go through it."

We are all drawn to partners who give us a chance to replay our primary dramas. But women choose men for more than their resemblance to their fathers—women also marry their mothers, and the men Molly picked allowed her to reenact her life with her mother as well as saving and being saved by her father.

She might have thought Richard's death a beautiful one partly because she was able to prove how loyal and brave she was in her love for him—how she could hang in, as neither of her parents were able to do with her. But also, by picking men who tend to tune out or become remote, she relives her life with her dazed mother—who also abandoned her in terms of parenting. But Terry, at least, tunes back in when Molly calls out to him. At the same time, he's responding to her ultimate wish—to be protected and cared for. She worries that a part of her would do anything—including becoming ill—in order to preserve a relationship. Since Molly's father was a physician, she was clearly calling out for him to come and save her. But this time she picked a man who answered that call.

Involuntary Service

Whether or not Molly actually requires relationships to be bonded by sickness, many people find themselves trapped in that role involuntarily. Spouses may become ill in a way that prevents them from being the partner we married. We want to believe that love will last through the hardest challenges, but we know it doesn't always: there are people who would argue that even a spouse who gains weight is no longer the person they married. As Molly points out, many people are not emotionally equipped to maintain intimacy with a dying spouse, and even those who want to are often too frightened. Being that close to someone who is dying makes them feel pulled into something they want to run from.

In cases where people are dying of a progressive disease, like multiple sclerosis, they may become so depressed or preoccupied with their incapacitation that they actually lose who they were, emotionally as well as physically, and their partner also loses the person he or she married. This state of affairs could go on for years and years.

Luckily, during Richard's illness Molly had a girlfriend and fellow Buddhist who kept her from falling into the hole. Many women have close friends whom they can lean on when their husbands become ill. Men often turn to a female lover when faced with a sick and dying wife.

It's an image that's commonly deplored—a man in bed with a healthy woman while his wife is dying of a terrible disease. But a man or woman who is losing his or her partner to a prolonged and depressing disease often wants someone to rescue him or her and help them through the ordeal. In part it brings up the problem of sacrifice: how to weigh your own needs for happiness against your obligations and promises to others—and what to do with the guilt or resentment, depending on your choice. Many people remain loyal and sacrifice their own happiness for years: some with continuing love, and others, with resentment. Some people just take off and leave—or put their partner in a nursing home. Still others arrive at some sort of compromise: they stay married but grant themselves the right to have an affair. None of these choices are simple, and the resulting conflicts or guilt get worked out in unconscious and frequently hurtful ways.

Molly's friend came to her rescue, but most people don't choose to get that close to death. Most of us are called on to play the part of rescuer at some point, but if this role is not in our repertoire, we're more likely to head for the emergency exit.

Frank was sixty-five when his wife, Carla, was diagnosed with multiple sclerosis. They had been fairly happy as a couple, but within two years, Carla was confined to a wheelchair, and she sank into a major depression. She lost all her interests in the world and other people. She barely spoke to Frank, except about her pains and medications. Frank was miserable—he was basically living alone, and he had no life outside work other than caring for Carla. Although a friend had suggested getting a divorce, Frank just did not feel he could divorce his wife after all these years, even though she was no longer the woman he had married.

He had fantasies of moving out and even checked the local real estate classified ads every day. He imagined himself living in one of those new downtown towers. This would be a good place to live as a bachelor, he thought: restaurants, dry cleaner, supermarket all within the complex. You could get everything you needed without putting on a coat. Or even have it delivered to your door. But Frank was inhibited by guilt and fear of what people would think of him.

Two years into Carla's illness, Frank decided he had a right to enjoy life, and that the only way he could stay with Carla was to have an affair that would give him the sexual and physical intimacy he needed. He assuaged his guilt with the thought that he could actually be a more caring husband to Carla if he had another relationship that met his needs and made him happy. He didn't really plan the affair— it just happened, and then he decided this choice was the fairest and best. He decided it would benefit everyone concerned and that nobody would get hurt.

His secret lover, Paula, worked in the office building where Frank was an accountant. She was fifty-six and had been divorced for several years. So Frank felt their affair was rewarding to Paula as well, because she wasn't involved with anyone else. She adored him and pampered him, cooking him wonderful meals, buying him underwear, and doing many of the things his wife could no longer do. She listened sympathetically to his daily reports of all the unpleasant things he had to deal with at home. Carla's illness had become so demanding, he felt he deserved every treat that Paula provided. And he felt that instead of taking care of only one woman, now he was making life better for two.

They'd spend the evenings in her apartment several times a week, and once in a while, Frank fabricated a business trip so he and Paula could get away for two days, leaving Carla in the hands of a professional caretaker. They spoke on the phone at least twice a day. Carla was in no position to complain, and she never said a word. If she suspected what was going on (and she probably did), Frank preferred not to know it. Neither Frank nor Paula had children, so no one else was keeping tabs on their whereabouts.

Things continued this way for seven years, when Carla suddenly died of a heart attack. Frank was surprisingly overcome with grief, and Paula, as usual, nursed him through his mourning period.

Since Frank had been declaring his love to Paula for years, she had assumed they would marry after a respectable waiting period. Of course, they had never actually discussed what would happen if Carla died, because Paula knew that Frank was not going to divorce her, and no one knew how long Carla was going to live.

Six months after Carla's death, Paula was devastated when Frank suddenly said he wanted the freedom to date other women! A few months later, she learned that Frank had already assumed that freedom well before his announcement. Finally he confessed he had met a beautiful and exciting younger woman—a fifty-seven-year-old businesswoman who looked more like thirty-five (Frank was then seventy-two and Paula was sixty-three). The company her late husband left to her was worth a fortune, and he believed this was the woman he was going to marry.

When Paula told Frank she was shocked and felt totally betrayed, Frank told her their relationship had been wonderful, and he didn't regret a moment of it, but they'd always known "in their heart of hearts" it wouldn't be permanent. When Paula asked why he never expected to marry her (it was certainly news to her), he told her that men always prefer younger women and that he and his new lover had more in common—the same level of education and shared interests in financial activities. Of course, she placed more demands on him than Paula had, and he complained that she could be controlling. He was still in the habit of looking to Paula for sympathy and consolation. When he left that night, Paula realized that she'd been an unpaid nurse and housekeeper for seven years.

When Paula had first started her affair with Frank, she was fifty-six. Now she was sixty-three, and her life had considerably narrowed since Frank had become the center of it. From time to time, afterward, she received a postcard from Frank, keeping her up-to-date on all his wonderful travels with his new wife.

There are people who might say that Paula got what she deserved, and she should have known that a man who would cheat on his wife would also cheat on her. In fact, Paula blamed herself for the total disaster and for being so stupid and naive.

This relationship had elements of several romantic scenarios and also shows how guilt can work in devious and destructive ways. Frank was guilty about having an affair when his wife was alive—or at least he worried about what people would think of him if they knew. But he had convinced himself during those years that his relationship with Paula was beneficial for everyone involved. As long as his needs for sex and company were being met, he was able to be a better husband to Carla. And since Paula wasn't otherwise involved, he felt he had given her love during many years she would have spent alone.

This was how Frank preferred to look at it, but some of his motives were not entirely conscious. Once Carla died, it felt better to start over with a clean slate. Marrying Paula would only remind him of his sins and his guilt. She had been a partner in his crime, and it would be better to erase her from the books. Marrying a new woman gave him a chance to put the past behind him. Of course, his new wife had other advantages too. But she would never have put up with seven years of serving him hand and foot.

Frank wasn't wrong in wanting to live when his wife was dying. He had a right to be happy, but he took advantage of Paula. Paula was foolish to think he'd ever stick around once he was free to start over again. If the widow hadn't turned up, someone else would have. If Paula had looked at the situation objectively, she would have known that Frank would want her to disappear the day after he buried his wife. She would always reflect his guilt, and he wanted a partner who would reflect his virtue.

During the relationship, Paula was engaged in some form of Rescue, because she was always consoling Frank over having to live with a sick wife. Like most rescuers she nurtured the hope that her wounded lover would one day be free to rescue her back. He would be the perfect husband to her after all the years she had cared for him.

Any woman who had taken an objective look at Frank would never have put herself in this situation. Afterward, Paula considered her seven-year affair with Frank to be the biggest mistake of her life. She wished she had spent those years finding a man she could marry and share her life with. But her error was not an isolated misjudgment—it was also related to her own fear of marriage. Like many women who unconsciously fear permanent commitments, Paula had denied that time was passing. This is the problem and romantic scenario we take up in the final chapter.

SELF-REFLECTIONS

1. You don't need to choose a partner who is dominated by serious deficits. If you are involved with someone who is seriously wounded, you might want to give up that person unless they show

clear signs that they will improve. If they choose to sink into their troubles, don't hold on or you'll go down with them.

2. Many people never fully recover from their early traumas—they'll be left with some degree of vulnerability. But wounds are more or less destructive. A man like Kelly's husband, Rich, who is a wonderful father and loving partner, may never be able to pay the bills. But still he is a gratifying partner, and Kelly was drawn to him for all his good qualities and because he let her be the one in control. That is totally different from a partner who exploits your love or treats you badly. The bottom line is this: does this person make you feel happier than you felt before, or does this person make you feel worthless or used?

3. If you have strong rescue tendencies, your ultimate wish is probably to be rescued yourself—to find someone to heal you as you would heal them. But you can't expect the person you rescue to turn into your own personal savior. A girl who grows up without a father always longs for that total protection she never received: the loving, invincible man who would rush headlong into a burning building to save his child, who would carry her out, unharmed by the flames. Often she displays the same unselfish courage or fierce determination in saving a wounded man. She does it because she hopes that, once he heals, she'll have recovered the lost father who would have protected her. If Rescue is your love story, you need to think of your valor as its own reward and not expect to be repaid in kind. While you do have a right to expect your love and care to be returned, your partner usually won't have the same fantasy you do. He probably won't model his behavior exactly on yours, so look carefully at what he does offer you and ask yourself whether it is enough.

❥

CHAPTER SEVEN

The Courage to Love: Overcoming Postponement and Avoidance

There is a land of the living and a land of the dead and the bridge is love, the only survival, the only meaning.

—THORNTON WILDER, *The Bridge of San Luis Rey*

The last of the love stories speaks to most of us and is probably the universal favorite. It tells of having the courage to risk a commitment to love and having the faith that love will survive every fear, separation, and obstacle. It's the story told in the movies *An Affair to Remember, Sleepless in Seattle,* and *Forever Young.* To reach the satisfying ending, a person needs to realize two things: they deserve to be happy and they don't have forever. And, of course, many people struggle hard with both of these.

The Courage to Love story usually involves people who habitually engage in two behaviors that prevent them from taking a chance on love: postponement and avoidance. These are the telltale signs of people who are afraid of commitment. Their lives seem to stay frozen in time, and they are sealed off from real engagement in the present world. Think of Miss Havisham in Dickens's novel *Great Expectations*. Long ago, she'd been left at the altar, and now, an old woman, she's still dressed as a bride, presiding over the petrified remains of her wedding cake. Many people are like Miss Havisham, although it's not immediately apparent to them or anyone else.

There are many different life experiences that can lead people to live this scenario: many avoiders of love were hurt before and don't want to risk being hurt again; postponers unconsciously equate making a commitment with aging and death; cynics focus only on their partners' flaws instead of looking within themselves and seeing that they are projecting their own self-hatred.

This scenario is not about falling easily into love. The hero and heroine must overcome internal fears that are even more formidable than the external obstacles that seem at first to be the problem. They face a tug of war between their wish to have love and their fears of commitment.

This story is also about the connections between love and death, and the desire for immortality. People who postpone and avoid love commitments are often living in a state of suspended animation—they are not moving forward but are often frozen in a time from their past. They believe that by delaying a commitment, they have stopped the clock. But like the Mel Gibson character in *Forever Young*, they learn that while they put things on hold, time had passed them by. Instead of preserving life, they lost it.

For people like this to change and open themselves to love, they must have a powerful shock that makes them see that it's really now or never. As long as people are comfortable living with the defenses they've constructed they don't have any motivation to change and they'll live as if they have forever. Only those who find the courage to risk love, with all its dangers, truly gain life and a kind of immortality.

Taking a Chance on Love: A World War II Story

Among the columns written by Ann Landers, some of the most popular are about people who had the courage to marry near strangers just before they were parted by World War II. Those stories are appealing to us because they're about people placing their faith in love rather than in fear. In my own family such a story involved my favorite uncle and aunt. They met in 1943, when they were both twenty-seven, just a few weeks before my uncle was shipping off to war in the South Pacific.

My aunt Shirley had worked for a few years after college and then joined the Women's Army Corps. She had just completed an officers' training program in Iowa and was heading to New York, where she was being stationed. When she got to Hartford, she took a short detour to visit her parents, who lived in a small nearby town. As she was boarding a local bus that went there, the driver of the express bus to Providence, Rhode Island, called out to her. He was an old neighbor and told Shirley to get on his bus—he'd make an unscheduled stop and get her home faster. So my aunt hopped on and sat in the front.

My uncle Arthur, just out of dental school, had enlisted in the army and was awaiting his assignment to be sent to the front to join a medical unit in some undisclosed location. He was about to leave his whole life behind and disappear into the war. At that time, soldiers weren't told where they were going, and even after they got there, they were ordered not to reveal their location in the letters they wrote home.

Arthur had been visiting his mother and sister (my mother) in New York, and now he was returning to his base in Providence. He had to change buses in Hartford, and when he boarded, he saw my aunt sitting there. She definitely stood out because female officers were rare. Curious, and always friendly, my uncle sat beside her, and they chatted for twenty-four minutes, until the bus stopped at my aunt's destination.

My uncle was intrigued, but they didn't exchange names or phone numbers because they never expected to see each other again. They were stationed 150 miles apart, and my uncle knew he would soon be shipping out for an indefinite period (as it turned out, he was sent to New Guinea for two and a half years).

Two weeks after that bus ride, Shirley stepped off a New York subway car at Pennsylvania Station, and my uncle accidentally collided with her. Surprised, they greeted each other like old friends. This time, my uncle asked for her name and learned that she was living in a hotel near the Waldorf-Astoria. Two days later, he came to New York with some army buddies. They wanted to meet girls and go dancing before leaving the country. My uncle called Shirley and left her a message, asking her to bring two friends and to meet him that night in the Hotel Pierre ballroom. She turned out to be a really good dance partner, and during the next two weeks, my uncle made several short trips to New York.

As his departure date approached, Arthur knew he didn't want to risk losing Shirley. So after two weeks of dating he asked her to marry him, and she said yes. Shirley's sister immediately posted an announcement in their local paper that Shirley and Arthur would marry in one week.

When my grandmother heard the news, she was distraught. It was bad enough that her son was going to war (and always the pessimist, she told my mother she didn't think she'd ever see him again), but she really couldn't stand the thought that he was choosing to marry. It appears the voluntary desertion upset her more. My grandmother's husband had died when she was a young woman (and when Arthur was twelve), and her son had been the focus of her life. Impoverished as a widow, seriously crippled from a childhood disease, and with no Social Security during the great depression, my indomitable grandmother had managed to scrimp and save so her son could have a good education and a secure occupation. She knew she couldn't stop the army from taking him, but she wasn't about to let him marry the "Connecticut Yankee."

My grandmother had succeeded before in breaking up Arthur's romances by always persuading him that he was too young to get married. Now she pleaded with him not to marry a stranger and threatened not to come to the wedding. This was very upsetting to my uncle because he'd always been a dutiful son.

Arthur was always a risk taker—racing motorcycles and flying small planes—which was probably a reaction to my grandmother's belief that something terrible was always about to happen. But he'd never defied his mother about anything important. He might have given in to her and postponed the marriage until he returned from war, but once he learned that the wedding had already been announced in a newspaper, he felt that calling it off would be too dishonorable.

Less consciously, he was also dying to get away from his controlling mother. Shirley could match his mother in strength and independence, but the two women were opposites in temperament, background, behavior, and appearance. He was afraid if he didn't marry Shirley right away, he might lose her. He had that critical *this is it* feeling. He had to take the risk.

People are often more open to falling in love when they are facing dramatic separation and loss. My uncle was heading into an unknowable future, in the company of total strangers, and leaving behind his entire world. It must have been easier for him to do that knowing he had someone to come home to, someone he belonged to. Shirley felt the same way. Even if my uncle died in the war, at least they would have lived.

Separation or a heightened awareness of mortality also makes people more willing to take risks. It doesn't happen only in wartime—many people who have always been too inhibited to make a romantic commitment fall in love after suffering a serious loss or learning they have a serious illness.

Even people who unconsciously equate commitment with being locked up probably are willing to take the risk when they are facing death. If they're going to be stuck in a coffin anyway, they might as well get married. Is it just a coincidence that people often use the same exclamation—this is it—when they think they're about to be in a fatal crash and when they fall in love at first sight?

There is also nothing like the immediacy of death—of someone we love, or the threat of our own—to remind us that we don't have forever. Until my uncle met Shirley, before leaving for war, he had always allowed his mother to make him feel guilty for wanting to leave her.

In the movie *Only the Lonely*, the guilty son lets his mother break up his engagement. But immediately after, he is shaken by the sudden death of a lifelong friend. His friend had also missed the chance for happiness and a family of his own because he couldn't leave his mother. When his mother died, he spent the rest of his life alone. His friend's death is the catalyst that transforms the hero, and he finds the courage to walk out on his mother and recover his bride.

My grandmother did go to Arthur's wedding, although she argued all the way through the ceremony, asking Shirley's father how he could let his daughter marry someone she hardly knew. "What's there to be afraid of?" he replied. "Your son seems like a very nice man."

Arthur and Shirley had thirty-one days together before they were parted for two and a half years. During World War II, you didn't get furloughs, and you couldn't make international phone calls from New Guinea. During this time, they wrote to each other every single day, and that was how they got to know each other. Years later, when they talked about that time, it never sounded awful (even though my uncle nearly died of malaria, which he didn't write home about). It seemed like an adventure, and my uncle never even recalled the horrors of war.

Arthur and Shirley were, and still are, a wonderful match. They're not worriers, and throughout their lives they brought an optimism to every problem they encountered, and things have always worked out well for them. Today, they are eighty-four years old and still deeply in love. They're more youthful than some people I know who are half their age. My uncle still croons the songs they danced to on their first date at the Pierre, and he goes to school reunions so he can show off his beautiful wife. Every day, he rides his bike and swims in the ocean. Their life is filled with lots of friends and with their children and grandchildren.

In contrast to those who believe they'll stay forever young if they postpone commitment, people like Arthur and Shirley who have the courage to take a risk when they meet the right person truly hold on to life and achieve immortality, as much as anyone can. They pack a lot into every day of their lives, and even after they die, they live on in the people they loved and who loved them.

Falling in Love after Confronting Mortality

It's not just in wartime that death opens up people to love and commitment. In the acclaimed recent novel by Melissa Banks, *The Girl's Guide to Hunting and Fishing,* the narrator, Jane, has avoided marriage well into her thirties, bouncing from one dead-end relationship to another. Only after her beloved father dies does she break up with Archie, her long-term lover, a much older man she was never going to marry.

Jane's long attachment to her older lover is obviously a Rescue scenario, tied to her fantasy of rescuing her father. For most of her adult life, her father has secretly suffered from leukemia. Jane has always been closer to him and had less respect for her mother, who is vague and less competent. During all the years her father was ill, Jane has been involved with a surrogate father. Archie is a renowned book editor, Jane's own profession. But although he's a mentor she admires in some ways, he's also an alcoholic and diabetic who refuses to face his problems or treat his illnesses.

There's an obvious tie between her lover and her father. Like the heroine of *Beauty and the Beast,* Jane runs back and forth between the two men as they lie critically ill, in different hospitals. Her father is far more noble. Even in his final hours, he worries about Jane and tries to help her. On the other hand, Archie acts like an infant and causes Jane to miss being with her father on the day her father dies. She knows, right then, that her relationship with Archie is over. Once her father is gone, the world feels different to Jane. She has lost the feeling of being watched over, which had always made her feel special.

One of the things we look for in love is that feeling of being watched over—a feeling we get most purely from our parents, if we are lucky. When a child says to her parent "look, look," and the parent responds with the right degree of interest and enthusiasm, the parent is really in tune with the child. That parent is capable of genuine empathy. Then the child feels watched over and loved—and this is the original basis for self-esteem. Later in life, love can reproduce that feeling of being watched over, to some degree, which is why love makes people feel connected to a vital source.

But when a parent responds to a child with a bored "okay" or "leave me alone, I'm busy" every time the child asks for recognition, the child does not feel very good about herself. Later in life, she will always be more vulnerable in romantic situations.

After her father's death, Jane leaves her job as well, because she no longer wants to put up with her (female) boss's abuse. She moves on to temporary jobs and to a younger boyfriend, but her problems aren't over. The new boyfriend is extremely self-absorbed and neurotic. Then Jane discovers a lump in her breast, and she stops living as if she had forever.

This is a major turning point. Now she's had cancer, as her father did, but her condition wasn't fatal. Will she keep squandering her own life, taking care of men who will never get better, or just let it slip away while she drifts from one temporary situation to another? She starts changing her life and is suddenly open to trying new things. At a friend's wedding, she meets the man who is right for her, and she chooses to live.

The Postponers

An Affair to Remember is the story of a couple (Cary Grant and Deborah Kerr in the most popular version) who have a shipboard romance, even while they are engaged to others. They promise to meet again—on top of the Empire State Building—after breaking off their (somewhat tenuous) engagements to others. This means a serious change for both, and they keep their promises.

Unfortunately, Kerr is delayed on her way to their reunion, and rushing to arrive on time, she is struck by a taxi and is left with paralyzed legs. Grant waits hours and hours for her in the wind and pouring rain until the building is closed. Kerr refuses to let him know why she never showed up because she's afraid he would marry her out of pity or guilt. The following Christmas, they accidentally cross paths and have a second chance. Their continuing love and a posthumous gift left by Grant's grandmother finally bring them together.

Most people who have seen *An Affair to Remember* recall the courage of the lovers—first, their willingness to change the course of their lives, then the heroine's courage to face her injury independently, and finally the couple's faith that everything will turn out well.

But few people notice that these lovers almost lose each other because of several unnecessary delays: first, their decision to wait six months before seeing each other again (did they really have to put their love to that kind of test?); second, the heroine's lateness (out of being polite to an old boyfriend) that leads her to rush in front of the car that strikes her; and finally, her decision to wait until she knows if she'll walk again before telling her lover what kept her from their meeting (why didn't she have more faith in his love?). The real wonder is that they finally get together, and they probably wouldn't have without the help of Grant's grandmother.

Most stories that end happily involve people who learn to seize the moment and embrace life by taking a risk. But what motivates those who delay? If some people feel that love is a way of facing down death, why do others feel that commitment is like being trapped alive in a box?

Postponement: Never the Right Time

Postponement is the story of Karen and Paul who are now in their mid-thirties. Karen works in an advertising firm, and Paul manages a sporting goods store owned by his father. They dated for almost five years and spent most evenings and weekends together. But they always maintained their separate homes—rent-stabilized apartments in Manhattan that they'd each held on to for over a decade. Their apartments were great deals (at a third of the market rate) and charming first homes for young singles. But neither apartment would have been adequate for Karen and Paul to share as a couple, and even as singles dwellers entering middle age, they had really outgrown these spaces and were living exactly the same way they'd lived right after college.

Paul wanted to get married and pressed Karen for a commitment. She always gave him the same we're-happy-as-we-are-why-do-we-need-the-piece-of-paper answer. Paul was anxious to start a family. He wanted to have several children, and he was starting to feel old. None of his friends were still single, and everyone close to him thought that Karen was using him until she found someone she really wanted to marry.

Finally Paul gave Karen an ultimatum—they should marry or

break up—and he accepted a compromise. Karen said he could announce their engagement, but she wasn't ready to set a date for the wedding. Paul was thrilled, and to celebrate the occasion he surprised Karen by renting a huge beach house for the Fourth of July weekend and inviting eighteen relatives and friends. He wanted to share his happiness with the people he loved.

Karen was annoyed with Paul's idea of fun. She thought he spent too much money on other people, and the idea of staying three days in a house filled with their relatives sounded like a nightmare. She angrily told Paul that he should have known she needed time and space for herself. He apologized for planning a surprise she might not have liked and volunteered to call it off, but Karen told him it was too late to do that; she'd just try to get through it.

Two nights before the start of the weekend, Karen woke up in a cold sweat and with chest pains. She thought she might be having a heart attack. She rushed to the nearest emergency room and spent the day going through a battery of tests. When she called Paul from the hospital to tell him how awful she felt, he didn't know whether to be furious or alarmed. The doctors soon decided that nothing was wrong with her; she was only having an anxiety attack.

That night she told Paul, reproachfully, that he'd have to stop pressuring her so much about getting married. The pain in her chest was a serious warning sign! She wasn't feeling physically up to the strain of the weekend party, but she encouraged him to go without her.

Paul felt deeply rejected and didn't see the point of going; it would be too painful. He had to call all the guests and tell them the weekend was off because Karen wasn't feeling well and needed to rest at home. They expressed concern for Karen and told Paul the party wasn't important, but privately they knew this meant Karen was never going to make a commitment. At this point, Paul finally realized it too.

Paul's friends despised Karen for stringing him along all those years, but truthfully, Paul's willingness to wait betrayed his own fear of commitment. Sometimes when we think that external forces are keeping us from having what we want, we actually need to look inside ourselves too. A person who waits and waits for external obstacles to clear, for a five-year lover to become ready for a commitment, is often the victim of his own self-deception. When someone waits too long for another person to allow them to start living, it often turns out that waiting was really that person's own choice.

Ha Jin's novel *Waiting* tells the story of Lin Kong, a doctor in China, who waits eighteen years to get a divorce so he can marry his colleague, Manna Wu, the woman he loves. Each year he returns to the traditional village where he was born to ask his wife and the local court for a divorce. Each year he is turned down and returns to the city and Manna Wu. Because he fears the Party's disapproval of adultery, his love affair with Manna Wu remains chaste.

Finally after eighteen years he gets his divorce and marries Manna Wu, but she's no longer the woman he thought he loved. Waiting for so many years has turned her into an angry, bitter woman. Lin Kong's first wife suddenly seems to be a lot more appealing than the woman he thought he wanted. After all these years, he couldn't remember why he wanted Mannu Wu.

Toward the end of the story he storms out of the apartment he shares with Manna Wu. He is startled when a loud disembodied voice confronts him. It challenges the illusions that have sustained him. The voice tells him he was willing to bow to obstacles and let them rule his life because that way he could believe he wanted what he couldn't have. Lin Kong isn't the only character in the book who has wasted his life waiting. His first wife and Manna Wu also lost the best years of their lives, waiting for Lin Kong to love them.

Forever Young: An Illusion

This is also the message of the movie *Forever Young*. Mel Gibson's character is a 1939 test pilot for the armed forces. He buys an engagement ring and is ready to propose to the girl he has loved since grade school. But when he tries to pop the question during their lunch date, he just can't get out the words. His endless stalling and small talk—trying to work up the courage—make his girlfriend late for work. Finally she rushes out to her job across the street, and borrowing from *An Affair to Remember,* is struck by a car and winds up in a coma. When she fails to wake up after several weeks pass, the doctors tell Gibson her condition is hopeless.

The hero can't stand the pain of losing the girl he has always loved, especially because he knows he unintentionally caused her accident by delaying her. His best friend, a scientist-inventor, has developed a secret method for putting animals into suspended animation by freezing them in nitrogen, and later thawing them back to life. Gibson is so depressed he begs to be the first human volunteer for the cryogenics experiment. Unexpectedly, the scientist has a heart attack and dies right after Gibson is frozen. Nobody else knows about the experiment, so the steel tank and Gibson are forgotten.

Fifty years pass, and two young boys sneak into a warehouse for discarded military equipment. Seeing the steel capsule, they play with its wheel, and suddenly a door flies open and a frozen man pops up. It's Gibson, a half century later, but looking not a day older than he did in 1939.

Eventually the hero discovers that his girlfriend didn't die after all—she came out of the coma soon after he'd gone into the capsule, and she never married. She is still alive, living in the same house where she lived as a child. Simultaneously, he discovers that his body has actually aged as well and is rapidly undergoing a metamorphosis through the fifty years it has been on hold. He rushes to get to his girlfriend's house before he dies, because he has no idea how long he was destined to live.

By the time he arrives, they are both eighty. She has also lived in a time capsule. Her life just came to a halt when she woke up and learned he'd mysteriously disappeared. After all this time, they are finally united. But his delay in proposing has cost them most of their lives—fifty years when their lives were not lived.

In *Forever Young,* the tragedy appears to be an accident, and we see their undying love surviving fifty years of separation. But it wouldn't have happened if Gibson hadn't taken so long to declare his commitment, or if he'd had a little more faith that she might recover, or if he'd had the courage to bear the pain of her injury a bit longer. If his courage hadn't failed, he would have been around when his girlfriend came out of the coma. But he'd been afraid to make the commitment, and later he hated himself too much to remain by her side to face the consequences. Upon waking, he is finally mature enough to open himself up to love, and at that moment, he loses his apparent immortality.

As long as he held himself back from committing to love, he appeared to be forever young, and once he gave himself over to love, age caught up with him. But he learns at the end that he could no more stop himself from aging than he could stop the passage of time. The idea that you can stay young if you put yourself on ice is always the great illusion.

In *Forever Young,* the heroine waits forever, and she's finally reunited with her true love. In real life, this rarely happens. In *My Best Friend's Wedding,* even Julia Roberts discovers that the boyfriend she spurned in college didn't wait around forever. She had always thought he would be there for her. They had once made a pact that if they hadn't married anyone else by the time they were twenty-eight, then they would marry each other. But just before Michael turns twenty-eight she finds out that he has, indeed, fallen in love with someone else—in fact, with a much younger woman, a college girl.

Like Lin Kong, the Julia Roberts character only thinks she wants what she can't have. At first she refuses to believe she has lost him, and she does everything possible to break up the marriage. By the time she finally declares her love, it's much too late. Maybe, she really didn't want him in the first place. But what are the psychological origins of the inability to commit?

For someone like the heroine of *The Girls' Guide to Hunting and Fishing* avoidance of commitment is somehow related to her attachment to her father; perhaps she feels guilty for not being able to save him from her mother. For someone like Karen, it's the terror of being boxed in, as well as her habit of always finding fault with other people instead of examining her own self-hatred.

People who accept themselves do not demand perfection in others, and therefore, they don't have as much trouble making a commitment to love. But a person with low self-esteem who can't face his own insecurities often projects his self-hatred onto other people and constantly focuses on the other person's flaws. If he could find a partner who was flawless, he could escape his self-hatred by merging with that perfection, and he may search the world for that perfection. But no one is perfect, and hating himself, he sees only flaws all around him and despises what he can't bear to see in himself. No one is ever good enough for such a person, and he cruelly reminds them of how they fall short. For these people, it's never the right time or the right place or the right person.

Onegin: The Cynic

Aleksandr Pushkin's novella-poem *Eugene Onegin* (recently made into a movie starring Ralph Fiennes) is about such a man. Outwardly, he's too cynical to love or make a commitment; beneath his contempt is self-hatred.

Prince Onegin is an aristocrat who gets bored with St. Petersburg society and moves to the country where he befriends Lensky, an idealistic neighbor. He also meets Lensky's fiancée, Olga, and her beautiful sister, Tatyana. The naive Tatyana becomes infatuated with the sophisticated Onegin, and she sends him a love letter. Initially, Onegin had been drawn by her beauty, but after reading her letter, he tells her that he can't return her affection. Soon after, at a party for Tatyana, Onegin flirts with her sister. It is probably jealousy of Lensky's happiness—common to many romantic cynics—that compels Onegin to prove that any woman, including Olga, can be easily seduced.

Outraged, Lensky challenges Onegin to a duel, to defend his fiancée's honor, and Onegin shoots and kills him. Afterward, Onegin withdraws from society.

Six years later, he returns to St. Petersburg, looking haunted. At a ball, he suddenly notices Tatyana, who has married his cousin, a wealthy and powerful prince. Not only is she more beautiful than before, and a princess, but she is even more attractive to Onegin because she is cool and unavailable.

Now the tables are turned, and Onegin is overcome with love for her. He pursues her obsessively, writing her love letters she never answers. He shows up anyplace she might be, even though she has made it clear that she doesn't wish to see him or speak to him. Finally, he breaks into her palace and, finding her alone, demands to know whether she still feels love for him.

All she will say in reply to his question is that she loved him once, but now he is too late. She is married to another man and will remain loyal to her husband. Onegin is left a broken man, walking the frozen streets of St. Petersburg like a ghost, waiting for a letter from Tatyana that never comes.

The story of Onegin is a brilliant portrait of the romantic cynic. Underneath his contempt for people who are unconflicted and loyal in their love is a man who despises himself and who finds fault with everyone else as a way of boosting his own low self-esteem. Onegin also needs to avoid any real intimacy because he's afraid that if anyone gets close enough, they'll see his flaws and reject him. He would rather reject them first.

The Cynic Returns

After Tatyana is married, he's obsessively drawn to her not because he really loves her, but because he wants to reassure himself that she's still in love with him. If he had truly loved her, he would have left her alone—she'd made it clear that she did not want any contact. But she has become the vision of perfection that he needs to merge with in order to feel complete. He persists because he needs to believe that he can defrost her, make her love him again, and thereby defrost himself. The man who returns too late doesn't return out of love for the woman he spurned. He comes back because he needs to know he can still inspire love.

Tatyana and her sister, Olga, made healthy decisions after their original romantic losses. After being hurt the first time, Tatyana has gained wisdom and married a man who adored her, and she has kept her commitment to him. Her sister, after mourning the death of her fiancé, met another wonderful man and made a happy marriage. Onegin alone was never able to feel love until he encountered a woman who didn't want him to come near her.

Women Who Accept the Abuse of Critical Men

As a rule, men like Onegin, cynical and hypercritical, often find women who allow themselves to be treated badly. Whenever the woman who loves such a man seeks some kind of reassurance or commitment, he responds cruelly as a way of undermining the validity of her requests. She takes this kind of abuse from a man because she has no sense of her own value that is independent of his opinion of her.

Sometimes her problem can be traced back to a father who treated her badly as a way of boosting his own self-regard. So she has gone from a father to a lover who behaves the same way. Often her mother suffered from low self-esteem too (for look at the man she married) and couldn't provide a healthier model for her daughter. Women who get involved with men like this often accept abuse for a very long time, never even confronting or questioning the man's behavior.

When the Tables Are Turned

The story of Onegin is also illuminating because it accurately describes what often happens to this type of man. Many men who go through several decades of criticizing flawed women often reach a point in life (around fifty) when they can't find a woman who will put up with them. They begin complaining that women are too demanding and critical, and they are the ones who get rejected because of their flaws. How does this reversal occur?

It would be nice to think that the women who took abuse in their youth finally developed greater self-respect. But probably what happens is that an aging Onegin is still pursuing beautiful young women, for only perfection will do. When he was young and did not have a long and terrible record, he could always find someone new. But at age seventy-five he's not likely to get a warm reception from young women who think he's laughable or pathetic. No wonder he thinks women are too critical—he's never taken a good look at himself.

Cynical Women

We often associate hypercritical, noncommitting behavior with men, but there are also female versions of Onegin; Karen, who kept finding faults in Paul, is one example. Nina is another, and her story suggests the origins of her behavior.

Nina is now twenty-seven, and the only relationship she's had that lasted more than six months was when she was in college, and this was with a French student who was returning home after his year abroad. Since then, she's been involved with a number of "impossible" men—just dating them rather than having any serious relationships. The reasons that made them "impossible" varied greatly: some were married, while others were so weak that they turned her off. In all of these affairs, she always felt relief more than sadness when they were over. In each case, the relationship felt more like an obligation than something she really enjoyed. She rationalizes her choice to be alone on the grounds that she needs independence and several outlets—and that any relationship eventually intrudes on this.

What made her this way? When Nina was eight, her father left her mother (and Nina as well). Unconsciously, Nina experienced her father's departure as a betrayal of her as a woman. She felt that he had cheated not just on her mother, but on her as well.

As a result, she identified with the aggressor and became more like a father, adapting an attitude that it's better to leave than to be left, and defending her behavior with a cynical perspective. Whenever she sees other people who are happy in love, she can't help but think how naive they are, and how they have no idea of the trouble and betrayal that is waiting for them around the corner.

"I assume men will cheat on me, so I think, why shouldn't I do it first? I have a belief in the inevitability of cheating or leaving, so I'd rather be the one who does it first. When I look at others who seem to be in love, I don't say it, but I always think, 'Boy, you don't know what you're in for.' "

In this way, Nina is much like Onegin at Tatyana's party—flirting with his best friend's fiancée to prove that she can't be trusted. She's not happy, so she can't bear to think that anyone else could be.

Nina's father actually came back to his marriage a few years after he left, and her mother took him back. But her words reveal that Nina has never forgiven him and feels that she was spurned. She neither identifies with nor respects her mother, who took him back. Her behavior suggests that, unconsciously, she was so hurt when her father left her that she'd prefer acting like him rather than putting herself in the position of being hurt again. She's highly critical of both her parents and doesn't enjoy spending time with either one. "I've gone from periods of forgiving my father, and then, not. He's never shown any remorse, no communication, nothing is talked about. My mom took him back and stayed in the marriage because it's safe—he's a constant. She doesn't seem to need any real intimacy—maybe she doesn't know what it is. I think he'd rather be alone and not home. He's never seemed to want to spend time with the family—he acts like he's forced to do it.

"I don't feel comfortable going home, although it makes my mother sad I don't visit. I've said to her, 'Why do you stay with him?' I've asked her what's wrong with him, and she says, 'Oh, that's just your dad.'

When asked why she's so afraid of intimacy, Nina accurately identifies the reason: "I'm afraid they won't like what they see."

How does she avoid being hurt?

"By not letting them control my time, refusing to be with them all the time. Or I don't call them back when they call me. I send subtle messages and try to avoid confrontations."

She doesn't examine her relationships at all. When asked why she didn't feel sad when a relationship ended, she replies, "I haven't processed it. I haven't asked what I learned. I just think what a loser he was." When asked if she's ever met a worthwhile man, she answers, "I think that if the relationship is right, all the cards will fall into place. You don't have to take inventory. It will just happen. If it's not meant to be, it won't be."

Nina defends her own noncommitment on the grounds that none of these men deserve it. So far, none of them has lived up to her standards.

She has more insight into her own behavior than Onegin did. She knows that at the core of her cynical attitude—her boredom with men—is a deep-seated sense of her own inadequacy. But she still prefers to find flaws in her partners rather than let them see hers. If they did, they might abandon her, as her father once did. Beyond admitting that fear, she resists "taking inventory" and examining her relationships.

Celia Vargas

Onegins appear on a continuum, with varying degrees of insight. Nina may be able to accurately describe her behavior, but she doesn't show much interest in changing it. She assumes there are only two positions in the world—the betrayer and the person who is betrayed. Given that choice, it's clear where she wants to be. In contrast, Celia Vargas, who is also in her midtwenties, more willingly examines her behavior.

Since college, Celia had always found a reason to break off relationships after they started getting serious and her boyfriends began to expect a commitment. She has never lived with a man full-time and has always kept her own apartment.

Last summer she traveled for a month with her current boyfriend, Doug, in Italy and Turkey. She found herself behaving in ways she didn't like or understand. For instance, she was constantly starting ridiculous arguments with him. All he had to do was wear a shirt that bothered her or repeat something he had told her before, and she would find a reason to blow up at him.

"We had never lived together, and I started to find all his domestic habits really annoying. He spent too long in the bathroom. It took him half an hour to shave. He had to find a newspaper every morning, and then he would spend an hour reading it, cover to cover. He was never ready to leave the hotel until about ten or eleven, and it made me furious. After a while, I started going off on my own in the morning while he was reading the newspaper. But I wouldn't come back when I was supposed to, so he had to sit around and wait for me. I did it on purpose because I felt he wasn't valuing my time. I should have told him what was bothering me, but instead I just made him wait longer and longer.

"Then I hated the way he snored. I'd poke him really hard, much harder than I needed to, to make him stop. But I found his snoring revolting and I wanted to hurt him. I told him I was totally exhausted because I didn't have one good night's sleep since we started our trip, all because of his snoring. It gave me an excuse not to have sex with him—I told him I was just too tired. I know he felt really bad about snoring, but he couldn't help it.

"I think I acted this way because I couldn't stand the intimacy of spending so much time together. We were totally trapped in each other's company for a month because we had no one else to talk to."

Celia must have known that traveling together could be difficult. Even couples who are used to living together can get on each other's nerves when they are together twenty-four hours a day. But Celia didn't give it much thought before the trip because she didn't want to picture how close they would be. By the time they got home, Celia was so turned off that she ended the relationship. Her boyfriend said he was really shocked and never expected it.

Celia's boyfriend was probably less surprised than he admitted. But he had accepted her behavior, pretending nothing was wrong, because he wanted to maintain the relationship no matter how she treated him. He probably didn't think that he deserved any better—like the women who put up with overly critical men. Some of his annoying habits might actually have served his own scenario of winding up rejected.

At least Celia is willing to look closely at her own behavior and acknowledge that she has trouble with intimacy, unlike Nina, who focuses on everyone else's weaknesses and thinks people are stupid if they expect to be happy. She took responsibility for her behavior after the fact, if not while she was with her boyfriend. This offers promise that she could act differently if she met someone she really wanted to be with.

Avoidance: Living in Retreat

Another reason that men and women avoid commitment is that they were badly hurt in love and never really recovered. They withdraw from love and sometimes from life, retreating into a pattern of fixed routines, in which there will be no unpleasant surprises. Nothing ever really happens in their life, and in that way, they are barely alive, even if they feel in control.

While they share certain features with obsessive lovers (allowing a romantic loss to wreck their lives), they are not as overtly angry, although anger is buried in there somewhere. Their outward behavior is more like calm resignation rather than aggression—they simply give up.

Usually people who get hurt to this degree by a romantic disappointment did not get much love from their parents. The romantic rejection mainly confirmed a more primal wound and caused them to give up hope. The heroine of Henry James's *Washington Square* is a good example. As I described earlier, Catherine's mother had died in childbirth and her father had always blamed her. When it seems she has finally found love, her father manages to prove that her suitor was only after her money. Catherine is deeply hurt by Morris's betrayal, but she's even more hurt that her father took such satisfaction in proving that her suitor didn't love her. She saw that he cared less about her happiness than proving that he was right.

After her engagement is broken, Catherine turns down several marriage proposals from worthy men and settles into spinsterhood, gaining a grim victory over her father. He thinks that the only reason why she wouldn't marry is that she and Morris are waiting for him to die so they can collect her full inheritance. Although she has no intentions of ever speaking to Morris again, she won't promise her father that she'll never marry him, and he disinherits her as a result. She doesn't need the money and prefers the victory of showing him that he can't control her with his money. She also decides she will never show him her feelings again.

After her father dies, she remains in the house where she was born, usually sitting in a rocking chair and embroidering. Twenty years after her heart was broken, Morris Townsend shows up without warning. He asks her why they can't just be friends and forget what has happened. Catherine had stopped thinking about Townsend a long time before, but his blindness to how much he hurt her draws out the feelings she had kept to herself all these years:"I can't forget. . . . I don't forget . . . You treated me too badly."

In contrast to those obsessive lovers who would kill themselves to show the world that their rejectors are murderers, Catherine preferred to keep her hurt feelings to herself. She blurts them out only because Townsend's intrusion into her quiet sanctuary took her by total surprise.

In the recent novel *The Romantics,* by the Indian writer Pankaj Mishra, the hero, Samar, also withdraws from the world after the only woman he loves leaves him after a brief affair. Like Catherine, he withdraws into routine and isolation, into an existence where he lives "neutrally on the surface," apart from the pain, pleasures, and desires that other people feel.

There are many ways to avoid love—withdrawal into a sealed-off existence is only one of many. Like Karen and Paul, many people also avoid serious commitments by investing all their energy and emotion on partners who are inaccessible or on relationships that could never become serious. Spending years on a long-distance relationship (in which you see someone a few times a year, with no plan to live in the same city) is another way to avoid meeting someone who might become a real partner. A similar avoidance strategy is living in the fantasy that a friend or a casual sex partner is really a lover.

The fear of intimacy is only one source of inhibition. Guilt is another. Some people develop avoidance patterns because, unconsciously, they feel their desires are forbidden.

Guilty: Avoiding the Forbidden

Sally, who is now twenty-six, was especially close to her brother John when they were growing up. Her parents were already quite old when Sally and John were born, and they never were physically affectionate with each other in front of their children. This often communicates some inhibition or prohibition about sex.

Sally has never really had a serious love relationship. She's had a few brief relationships with men, but the attraction was primarily sexual—and the affairs consisted of a few nights in bed. They were all men Sally found attractive, and the one thing Sally feels most insecure about is her sexual attractiveness. So these affairs boosted her self-image as a sexual, desirable woman.

Unfortunately, the men lacked all the other qualities she looks for in a man. What she is looking for is her "shadow"—a man who shares her emotional and spiritual qualities, a man with a sense of humor and playfulness, a man with whom everything would be equal. And she adds, incidentally, that these are all qualities that she sees and appreciates in her brother, John.

She's had many crushes that were never requited. Typically, she meets someone at work who becomes a friend, and then she finds herself attracted and hopes her friend will return her feelings. It doesn't happen. Then she blames herself for not being the person he wanted. Why does she think it doesn't happen?

"I don't know. It's as if men put you into one category or another—friend or lover—and once you're a friend they can't have sexual feelings for you. Your roles become fixed. A couple of times I've said to a friend I'm attracted to that I think there's something more there. And they both said, 'No, I'm sorry.' I guess I'm not a good judge—I don't read the signs and signals correctly, I misread people. When I push the limit, I discover I was wrong."

Although Sally explicitly states that she's looking for her "shadow" and someone who is just like her brother, what she doesn't recognize is that she is searching for a forbidden, taboo object. It's not that she actually wants to be her brother's lover, but unconsciously she feels that her desires are taboo. And as a result she splits sex from love and has trouble putting them together.

She has sex with men she doesn't feel close to, and she keeps repeating the scenario of falling for friends who wouldn't have sex with her because she's in the "wrong" category. When she complains about friends who can't see her in a sexual way, she is really project-ing her own inhibitions, because she has split sex from love. By hav-ing unrequited crushes on male friends who aren't interested in her, and inviting their rejection, she also punishes herself for wanting someone like her brother, who is taboo.

A more common source of punishment occurs when parents haven't given you permission to have love. It's not something a per-son is usually conscious of, but it has a tremendous impact. If your parents make you feel that you don't have the right to fall in love, one common response is to break away from them and their control, but that is often accompanied by the need to punish yourself for breaking the taboo—perhaps by picking partners who treat you badly.

In the movie *Crossing Delancey* the heroine (Amy Irving) is trying to escape from her family, but she's having a hard time because her parents apparently didn't give her permission to be happy in love. She rebels against her parents by choosing men who are different from the ones she grew up with. But the guilt she feels about this rebellion causes her to get into relationships that go nowhere—with men who use her. She reenacts the crime of leaving her parents and takes her own punishment.

While visiting her grandmother on the Lower East Side of Man-hattan, she meets a man (Peter Riegert) who treats her well. He has no conflicts about wanting her, but she can't respond and she mistak-enly thinks it's because he's from the world that she left behind. In fact, the reason she's not attracted to him has nothing to do with where he's from; he's a taboo object because any real happiness would make her feel guilty.

The man who pursues Irving sells sour pickles on the Lower East Side—a business he inherited from his father. Irving works in an uptown bookstore, where she's underpaid and exploited by her employer and the narcissistic literati who gather there. But her association with this world has given her an identity separate from her parents.

The pickle man (who is extremely perceptive and a great deal wiser than the heroine) correctly sees that Irving is incapable of being attracted to a man who will treat her decently. He doesn't have problems with his self-esteem, so he can be unconflicted about his attraction. This is also why he doesn't think he's been rejected because he's truly unworthy.

Showing a healthy attitude, he decides to move on to a woman who doesn't have Irving's problems, one of her best friends, whom she had arranged for him to meet. When Irving discovers how much her friend likes the man she'd rejected, she starts to question her original reaction and begins to see him in a whole new light. Eventually, because her grandmother encourages this match, giving her the permission to be happy that she apparently never got from her parents, the taboo is lifted, and she's free to love a man who will love her back.

Getting over Delay or Avoidance: The Second Chance

What does it take to penetrate the fantasy that you have forever to find love? A close encounter with death is the blow that does it for some people. The return of an old lover is another common catalyst: the shock of it not only puts postponers in touch with their younger selves, when they were open to love, but it also makes them painfully aware of the gap between then and now. This can break through an adaptation of avoidance—a person who thought their chance for love had come and gone may reach out and grab a second chance for happiness.

Jane Austen's novel *Persuasion* (and the recent movie version) tells the story of Anne Elliott who fell in love with the right man at the age of nineteen. He'd loved her at the time and asked her to marry him. But sadly, she had taken the advice of an older woman to reject his proposal because Captain Wentworth had no money and, therefore, was not the "right match" for her. In turning him down, she had silenced her own feelings and her own voice. After that, years passed, and no other match occurred.

As a spinster in early-nineteenth-century England, the heroine occupied a dreaded position in society. She had to depend on the good will of others, which meant she was rarely allowed to speak, because being unmarried, she didn't count. She could only play the role of the sympathetic listener to people whose thoughts and sentiments were far less developed than her own.

Years later, Wentworth returns from a long absence at sea. Now he is rich and handsome—he's become the captain of an important ship—while Anne has faded so drastically that he barely recognizes her. At first, she watches silently from the sidelines as Wentworth is pursued by younger women—because now he's the most sought-after man in town. He rarely looks at or speaks to the heroine. But the shock of seeing what she has lost brings her back to life. Her pallid complexion acquires a healthier color and glow. She finds the courage finally to speak out. The hero sees all the qualities in her he once loved and still loves, and they have their second chance.

Sometimes it just makes a difference to know that we were never forgotten by someone we loved long ago. This happened to Grace Caravaggio. On the day she turned fifty-five she received a birthday call from John Cowan, a man she had loved in her youth. He had ended their affair because she was Catholic and his Protestant parents had talked him out of marrying her because of their religious differences. Although Grace had been crushed by John's betrayal, she had recovered and married someone else, like Tatyana in Pushkin's *Eugene Onegin*. But she never felt the same kind of passion for her husband that she'd felt for the man who broke her heart, and the marriage had not made her husband happy either.

John had moved to England, and for thirty years he and Grace had had no contact. Then on a visit to Chicago, John tracked down Grace and asked to see her. Grace declined the invitation, perhaps wisely. John was merely curious and thought it would be interesting to see what had become of her. But Grace could interpret his call after thirty years as evidence that he'd never really gotten over their separation. She felt a little bit that this evened the score, and it made her feel better.

Why, after a thirty-year absence, would a man look up a woman whose heart he had broken? It's usually not because he's recognized his error and really loved her all along, as Grace preferred to think. He might just be feeling some vague sense of loss and need to connect with a figure from his youth. Sometimes it's because he has suffered some blow to his self-esteem, so he returns to a woman he rejected to see if he can still inspire love—as Onegin did. Or he returns to a woman who loved him once because he wants to know that he hasn't been forgotten, and not because he's any more capable of loving her.

A Scoundrel Returns

Grace Caravaggio's life was not transformed by hearing from John. It usually takes a deeper, more painful encounter to activate a significant change. A scoundrel's return that does have this impact is the theme of Elinor Lipman's recent novel, *The Ladies' Man*. The author has said that this story was inspired by something that really happened in her family eighty years ago.

Lipman is often described as a contemporary Jane Austen in her themes and her style. This novel, like Austen's *Persuasion,* concerns a woman whose life came to a halt after a broken marriage engagement. In 1967, when she was in her early twenties, the heroine's fiancé failed to show up at their engagement party at the Boston Copley Plaza Hotel. By the time anyone knew he was missing, he'd already flown to California.

The heroine is fifty-three-year-old Adele Dobbin, an attractive, professional woman who has carefully avoided any romantic entanglements since that terrible night. Adele was pretty and intelligent, and after the fiasco of her runaway groom, everyone had always said she would meet someone new, but she never did.

In her twenties and thirties she had rejected several reasonable suitors; by the time she was forty, the available men fell a far greater distance from the impossible standard she had set. By the time the novel opens, Adele had concluded it was too late for her to have many of the things she wanted.

She lives with her two sisters near Boston's Beacon Hill. The Dobbin sisters were all attractive, and many people wondered why none of them married; they suspected it was related to the broken engagement from thirty years before. Adele insisted that she'd gotten over Harvey immediately and was thankful she was spared from the marriage. But the Dobbin sisters live in something of a time capsule that protects them from real life.

For the past thirty years the last one to bed would turn all the locks and line up the same ten empty soda bottles they'd been using for decades as an alarm system to alert them to intruders. The ritual dated back to the 1960s, when the Boston Strangler was on the loose, but the sisters maintained the precaution because they'd been taught to prepare for the worst.

Their vigilant world is upset when Harvey Nash appears at their door, without warning, thirty years after he'd disappeared. He's been living with a woman in California. To escape his current partner, Harvey has now run off to Boston. He hasn't changed a bit. He's still a compulsive ladies' man, unable to get through a single day without finding a new woman to exploit.

Harvey's return brings unaccustomed pain and humiliation to Adele, after she has spent the intervening years avoiding vulnerability and life. But that kind of pain can be a catalyst for dramatic change, and it transforms Adele's life as well as her sisters'. Adele had thought it was too late for anything to change, and she had settled into a life that seemed comfortable and safe.

Harvey's reappearance and all the old wounds it reopens forces the Dobbin sisters to face how much of their lives have slipped by and to realize that they don't have another moment to lose. Suddenly they are reexamining their values and finding love they hadn't expected.

It may seem like a contrivance when movies or novels build their plots around dramatic events like the return of a long-lost lover, or a wrong wedding stopped at the last moment so the right one may take place (*The Philadelphia Story, Four Weddings and a Funeral*), or a love that is seized only after the protagonist confronts her mortality and must choose between life or a living death. But these plots never grow old because they tell profoundly true stories about love that most of us can relate to: the dangers of avoidance or postponement, and finding the courage to claim your life and the one you love.

Avoidance and Recovery

One of the most moving films ever made about avoidance and recovering from lost love is *Red*, the last part of a trilogy by the late Polish director Krzysztof Kieslowski. The young heroine of the film, a model named Valentine (Irene Jacob), is living a life of avoidance through her long-distance romance with a boyfriend she rarely sees. She mostly talks to him on the telephone instead of having a real relationship.

One night, while driving in the rain, Valentine accidentally strikes a dog, but it recovers. The next day she returns it to the address on its collar. It belongs to a retired judge (Jean-Louis Trintignant), an uncommunicative recluse who seems to be totally indifferent to his dog or to anything else. His only interest is spying on his neighbors and secretly tapping into phone conversations.

Valentine is appalled by his behavior, but she keeps returning to him and the (pregnant) dog, and the two love-avoiders discover a deep connection. The retired judge changes—he gives up his spying and opens himself emotionally to Valentine. We learn that he never recovered from a cruel romantic betrayal when he was a young man. Since then, he had related to people only as a distant observer of their infidelities and crimes—first in his professional life as a judge, then in his own illegal practices as a voyeur.

One person the judge has been spying on is a young reincarnation of himself. Auguste is a new judge who experiences a romantic betrayal identical to the one that had wrecked the older judge's life. He lives across the street from Valentine, but they have never met.

The old judge has long made a practice of never getting involved in human affairs, but when Valentine tells him of a trip to England she is planning, he tells her not to fly across the English Channel, but to travel by ferry instead. Auguste, his younger alter ego, will be on the same boat.

While Valentine is gone, the judge's dog gives birth to puppies, and he is playing with the one he has chosen for Valentine when he learns of a tragic accident. He stares at the television report. The ferry carrying Valentine and Auguste had been caught in an unexpected storm and has vanished into the icy waters, a terrible catastrophe at sea. There were 1,435 passengers, and only seven have been recovered alive. The judge watches, transfixed, as the camera zooms in on the few survivors; the two people he loves do not appear to be among them. We wait an agonizing moment with him, and finally, the camera sweeps toward the last surviving pair—Valentine and the young judge, wrapped in blankets, shivering and wet. We see from their expressions that they will fall in love with each other and marry.

It's a heartbreaking moment in the film when we're reminded that loving someone leaves us terribly exposed to the anguish of losing them. It had happened to the hero once and appeared to be happening again. Even worse, we feel the horror of knowing you can unintentionally cause injury or death to the person you love the most.

Red, like all of Krzysztof Kieslowski's films, tells a captivating story about the forces of chance and accidental connections. If the old judge had been forty years younger he and Valentine might have married, but they were separated by time. In a moment, an accident took hundreds of lives and almost robbed the judge of the people he loved.

If my aunt had not switched buses at the last moment in Hartford, and my uncle had not collided with her two weeks later on a subway platform in New York, and my aunt's sister had not placed the wedding announcement in the newspaper, then my uncle and aunt never would have married. If their children were telling the story, they'd probably add, "And then we wouldn't have been born." This is why some children never tire of hearing the story of how their parents met and fell in love: it's the story of how they got to be born. And given the odds against everything happening as it did, they recognize their birth as the miracle it is.

A chain of remarkable events appears in almost every love story, which adds to the feeling that love is a miracle, or the result of some divine plan. Seeing the power of random events in life can either make us feel powerless or make us feel those events must have been preordained, since the odds of their happening were infinitely small. Accident or fate, either way, it seems beyond our control. Still we exercise final control because our lives are the choices we make in response to everything that comes our way. Even with all those accidental connections lined up in their favor, my uncle and aunt still would not have married if my uncle had chosen to let his mother have her way.

The most powerful moment in *Red* is when the judge stares at the television screen to learn the fate of Valentine and Auguste. He is facing the fear and pain of loss that go with risking love after years of turning away from it. He resisted having his heart broken again, he took a chance, and his heart may break again. We've also seen the emptiness in his life that came with avoiding the risk. That is the central dilemma of this love scenario.

The retired judge was too old to marry Valentine, but love has brought him back to the living and given him a second chance to be happy. The judge has brought Valentine together with the man who represents his younger self and whom the judge has grown to love. Auguste and Valentine might have died, but they didn't. And the judge has gained two surrogate children to take the place of the ones he missed having in his wasted years. He's brought them together, where he knows they belong. Second chances do come, but only to those who accept that you don't avoid death by protecting yourself from life.

SELF-REFLECTIONS

1. Do you tend to focus on the flaws in the your partner or your potential partners? Have you considered that this may be a reflection of feeling inadequate yourself?

2. Have you always become involved with people who are unavailable, or live out of town, or will never be committed to you? If you aren't sure about how serious they are about you, do you ask them questions that will give you the answers? Have you withdrawn from life and love because you were hurt before?

3. Do you tend to postpone commitments in relationships, or are you involved with someone who has kept you waiting for a long time because he's not ready for a committed relationship? If so, are you denying that time is passing?

4. What do you really want in life, and how much time do you think you have to get it? Are you wasting so much time that you are letting your chance to have those things slip away?

♥

CHAPTER EIGHT

Conclusion:
How to Choose Your Happy Ending

Changing you primary love story is almost as impossible as trying to change your past. Your romantic inclinations will probably always be with you, but you can change the way your plot develops. As you have seen, within any story some people find great happiness while others merely try to survive. The choice of which way your story turns is up to you. In the cult film *Scream,* the leading male character concludes that life is just like a movie, except that we don't get to pick our genre. But he's wrong. We don't choose our story, but we *can* change its genre.

Here are some ideas to remember. They'll help you to make the best choices in any of the Seven Stories.

1. If your parents didn't give you permission to separate from them and leave them, find someone else (your peers or a parental substitute) who will help you feel you have a right to your own happiness.

   If your parents made you feel your happiness was injuring them, find someone you trust and respect who will tell you that it's okay: for example, a friend who lived through the same problem, and whose parents survived and adapted.

2. As I've pointed out, most of us are drawn to one particular story, but if you find yourself constantly repeating one or find yourself in an extreme version of one, you are probably picking the wrong partners. With these lovers you are reliving your old trauma. Instead of growing beyond it, you're merely confirming your worst fears. The question is why?

Your connection to your story is probably so intense that you choose partners primarily based on their resonance with your original problem. But successful relationships require other things beyond trauma repetition. You need a partner with other good qualities who also shares your interests and values.

3. This doesn't mean you should settle for someone who bores you. You may meet someone perfectly wonderful—the kind of guy everybody wants to marry—but he puts you to sleep. It's much more exciting for you to be with someone who doesn't look as perfect on paper. The latter probably fits into your primary scenario while the former does not. Whether someone fits with our story is often the difference between boredom and excitement.

Your friends and relatives will probably assure you that your passion will grow over time for the perfect guy who doesn't fit your story. But let's face it: if you don't think he's interesting now, it's unlikely that you'll find him interesting five years from now. That's why in *Sleepless in Seattle* Meg Ryan knew she had to break off her sensible engagement to follow her heart.

Besides, the perfect but boring guy probably has a story of his own, which you didn't notice because it didn't interest you. It might start to irritate you once you see it.

There's probably an optimal degree to which a partner should resonate with your story. If that connection is entirely

missing, the relationship may always feel flat. But if his resonance with your story is too intense, the relationship will
probably turn out badly. The most satisfying unions involve a
partner who fits into your story constructively, a partner who
in addition to having qualities you admire helps make your
story come out better.

In other words, *Don't try to fight your story.* Accept it. It is
part of who you are and it addresses your needs.

4. So how can you tell who will make you happy? It's really
    essential to see your partner as objectively as possible and to
    make an honest assessment of his capacity to love you.

    Ask yourself these questions: what has he achieved in
    work and love, but especially in love? Have his prior relation-
    ships been positive and successful?

    If you've read this far, you are obviously trying to look at
    the internal sources of your problems, instead of always blam-
    ing external factors. You want a partner who will do the
    same—someone who will take responsibility for his own prob-
    lems. Don't blame yourself for everything that goes wrong.

    Ask yourself, Which of the scenarios does he follow, and
    how many times has he repeated it? Is this a story you can
    live with? If he keeps repeating the same scenario, he's prob-
    ably not a good choice, unless he's gained insight into his
    own behavior.

    Ask yourself whether he's likely to help you overcome
    your fears, or if he is likely to arouse them.

5. You can usually tell that you've chosen the wrong partner if
    he makes you feel more pain, anxiety, and depression than
    you felt before you got involved with him.

6. If you are feeling anxious in a relationship, you should also
    face the internal sources of your discomfort. If your fears are

coming from your own sense of inadequacy, deal with them independently, outside the relationship. If you do, you'll be in a better position to judge whether this lover or the next one is the right person for you.

7. If you keep repeating unhappy scenarios, then in addition to assessing your partners honestly, you need to look at your relationships accurately. Review your repetitive history and ask yourself whether your relationships were really the way you remember them, or were your perceptions distorted?

In the movie *High Fidelity*, the narrator (John Cusack) has just been dumped by his latest girlfriend, repeating the pattern of his love life as far back as grade school. He wonders why the same thing keeps happening and decides to look up each of these women to get their view of what went wrong.

What he learns is that things didn't happen the way he remembered them. Most of the time, he wasn't really abandoned—in fact, he usually engineered the breakups. As his perception is corrected, he sees his behavior more honestly. He realizes that he drove his most recent girlfriend away, and that he really wants to be with her. Having changed, he's able to win her back.

In real life, it probably won't work to ask old lovers for their view of what happened (though aren't we often tempted?). What they'll remember probably has more to do with their own stories.

But you can talk about your repeated scenarios with your current partner. In fact, you should. It's a way of assessing whether this person is someone who will help you overcome your fears. It's also a good opportunity to ask them about their own scenarios and to learn as much as you can about this person. It's a good idea to know that you haven't picked someone who is stuck on repeating their own disappointments.

8. Lovers don't always have to love each other equally. Often one person is more loving than the other, and that doesn't necessarily harm the relationship. One person may not need to be loved as much as the other, because giving love may be gratifying too. Some people are more comfortable being the lover rather than being the passive recipient (this is often true of male rescuers), and some people feel less vulnerable in the role of the giver. What really matters is that the partners' needs are complementary, and to achieve that each person's needs don't have to be the same.

9. Just as lovers don't have to love each other equally, the partners may not be living out the same love story. For example, David Stewart's story was Sacrifice, while Kim Carlson's story was Upstairs-Downstairs. But partners' scenarios must fit together in a way that is mutually beneficial and raises both partners' self-esteem. Relationships that make only one person happy won't be as strong or as satisfying.

10. Don't expect your story to come to a final or complete resolution, even if you find the right partner. Your story will always be a part of you. It will resurface from time to time in a form that's somewhat different or even disguised. Once you understand your story, you'll be better at recognizing its patterns and will be able to exercise better choices and control.

11. Our stories may lie within us forever, but relationships change, sometimes after a partner's needs have been met. If you are the first love of someone who chose you because you could help him break away from his or her parents, don't be surprised if he or she moves on from you after you've fulfilled your purpose. This is one reason you need to be aware of

your partner's love story. If it was predictable that your relationship wouldn't last, try not to blame anybody, especially
yourself. This was understood by the realistic hero in *Dirty
Dancing*. If someone has rescued you when you were needy
and depressed, and you know he has a history of saving
injured women, don't be surprised if he finds you less attractive once you grow into a strong and independent woman.

12. Time never stands still, even if you are a postponer and have
avoided love. Avoiding commitment or going into hibernation doesn't keep us young. In *My Best Friend's Wedding*,
Julia Roberts isn't able to halt the wedding ceremony, as
other film heroes have managed to do. If you don't have the
courage to act when it's necessary, you might lose that person forever. But it's never too late to find love with somebody else.

   If you have withdrawn from relationships altogether
because of previous romantic disappointments, and you've
given up on finding love, you need to ask yourself why you
are avoiding involvement. Instead of seeing yourself as a person who life has passed by, think about all the ways you've
caused this.

   Of course it's harder for women to find partners after
they're no longer young, but people who really want to find
love often do—at every age.

   Remember Adele Dobbin, Elinor Lipman's heroine, who
finds love at age fifty-three after having withdrawn for thirty
years. Once she gets over her fear of looking foolish, she finds
herself wildly attracted to a man who had always been
around, right in her own backyard.

   People, old and young, who have lost someone they
loved often keep love at bay by insisting that only the lost
one will do. They see only flaws in the person who is pres-

ent because anyone different from the lost one reminds them of what they have lost, and this arouses their anger. Once they are willing to open their hearts, they often discover the new partner is actually vastly better than the one they had before.

You can't replace the years you lose when you get trapped in an ancient scenario, any more than you can bring a dead person back to life. But it's also true that as long as you are alive, it's never too late to find the happy ending for your story.

References

Movies

Affair to Remember, An (1957) Leo McCarey, director

All About Eve (1950) Joseph Mankiewicz, director

Annie Hall (1977) Woody Allen, director

Beauty and the Beast (1946) Jean Cocteau, director

Beauty and the Beast (1991) Gary Trousdale, director

Belle de Jour (1967) Luis Buñuel, director

Bridges of Madison County, The (1995) Clint Eastwood, director

Brief Encounter (1945) David Lean, director

Casablanca (1942) Michael Curtiz, director

Chasing Amy (1997) Kevin Smith, director

Coming Home (1978) Hal Ashby, director

Crossing Delancey (1988) Joan Micklin Silver, director

Damage (1992) Louis Malle, director

Dark Victory (1939) Edmund Goulding, director

Dead, The (1987) John Huston, director

Dirty Dancing (1987) Emile Ardolino, director

Educating Rita (1983) Lewis Gilbert, director

End of the Affair, The (2000) Neil Jordan, director

Eugene Onegin (2000) Martha Fiennes, director

Eve's Bayou (1997) Kasi Lemmons, director

Fatal Attraction (1987) Adrian Lyne, director

Forever Young (1992) Steve Miner, director

Four Weddings and a Funeral (1994) Mike Newell, director

High Fidelity (2000) Stephen Frears, director

Horse Whisperer, The (1998) Robert Redford, director

Marty (1955) Delbert Mann, director

Mona Lisa (1986) Neil Jordan, director

Mr. Jealousy (1998) Noah Baumbach, director

My Best Friend's Wedding (1997) P. J. Hogan, director

My Fair Lady (1964) George Cukor, director

Now, Voyager (1942) Irving Rapper, director

Officer and a Gentleman, An (1982) Taylor Hackford, director

Only the Lonely (1991) Chris Columbus, director

Peggy Sue Got Married (1986) Francis Coppola, director

Philadelphia Story (1940) George Cukor, director

Play Misty for Me (1971) Clint Eastwood, director

Pretty Woman (1990) Garry Marshall, director

Rebecca (1940) Alfred Hitchcock, director

Red (1994) Krzysztof, Kieslowski, director

Return to Me (2000) Bonnie Hunt, director

Roman Holiday (1953) William Wyler, director

Run Lola Run (1998) Tom Tykwer, director

Saving Private Ryan (1998) Steven Spielberg, director

Scream (1996) Wes Craven, director

Sleepless in Seattle (1993) Nora Ephron, director

Titanic (1997) James Cameron, director

Twice in a Lifetime (1985) Bud Yorkin, director

Way We Were, The (1973) Sydney Pollack, director

What Dreams May Come (2000) Vincent Ward, director

What's Love Got to Do with It? (1993) Brian Gibson, director

Wonder Boys (2000) Curtis Hanson, director

Working Girl (1988) Mike Nichols, director

You've Got Mail (1998) Nora Ephron, director

Books

Aristotle. *Poetics*, trans. Ingram Bywater, in *Introduction to Aristotle,* ed. Richard McKeon. Chicago: University of Chicago Press, 1973.

Austen, Jane. *Persuasion* and *Pride and Prejudice.* New York: Dover Press, 1997.

Brontë, Charlotte. *Jane Eyre* in *Three Great Novels.* Oxford: Oxford University Press, 1994.

Brontë, Emily. *Wuthering Heights* in *Three Great Novels.* Oxford: Oxford University Press, 1994.

Banks, Melissa. *The Girls' Guide to Hunting and Fishing.* New York: Viking Press, 1994.

de Beauvoir, Simone. "The Woman in Love" in *The Second Sex.* New York: Vintage Press, 1994.

Dickens, Charles. *Great Expectations.* Oxford: Oxford University Press, 1987.

du Maurier, Daphne. *Rebecca.* New York: Avon Books, 1997.

Fowles, John. *The Collector.* New York: Little Brown, 1997.

Gordon, Mary. *Seeing through Places.* New York: Scribner, 2000.

———. *The Shadow Man.* New York: Vintage, 1997.

Gornick, Vivian. *Fierce Attachments.* New York: Beacon, 1997.

Hugo, Victor. translated from "Booz endormi," in *La Legende des Siecles.* Paris: Garnier, 1962.

James, Henry. *Washington Square.* New York: Viking Press, 1985.

Jin, Ha. *Waiting*. New York: Pantheon/Random House, 1999.

Johnson, Diane. *Le Divorce*. New York: Plume, 1998.

Joyce, James. *Dubliners, including The Dead*. New York: Modern Library, 1993.

Lipman, Elinor. *The Ladies' Man*. New York: Random House, 1998.

Malcolm, Janet. *The Crime of Sheila McGough*. New York: Alfred A. Knopf, 1999.

Margulies, Donald. *Collected Stories— A Play*. New York: Theatre Commission Group, 1998.

Maynard, Joyce. *At Home in the World: A Memoir*. New York: Picador USA, 1998.

Miller, Sue. *While I Was Gone*. New York: Ballantine, 2000.

Mishra, Pankaj. *The Romantics*. New York: Random House, 2000.

Person, Ethel. *Dreams of Love and Fateful Encounters*. New York: Penguin USA, 1989.

Rose, Phyllis. *Never Say Goodbye: Essays*. New York: Doubleday, 1990.

Spencer, Scott. *Endless Love*. New York: Alfred A. Knopf, 1979.

Tennyson, Alfred Lord. "The Day-Dream," in *The Poetic and Dramatic Works of Alfred, Lord Tennyson*. Boston and New York: Houghton Mifflin and Co., 1899.

Tolstoy, Leo. *Anna Karenina*. New York: Bantam Classics, 1984.

Waller, Robert James. *The Bridges of Madison County*. New York: Warner, 1992.

Wilder, Thornton. *The Bridge of San Luis Rey*. New York: Grosset and Dunlap, 1961.

Yalom, Irvin D. *Love's Executioner*. New York: HarperCollins, 1990.

Acknowledgments

To Wayne A. Myers, my brilliant friend and teacher, I owe a debt too vast to describe. His imagination and profound understanding of relationships are the source of what is best in this work.

Sandra Dijkstra, my extraordinary agent, was a vital force in conceptualizing this book, and all through the process.

I thank Henry Ferris, my editor at William Morrow, for his dedication, good judgment, sense of humor, and for the countless ways he has helped me.

I am grateful to Paul Bresnick for placing his faith in this project when it was just beginning. F. Robert Stein, Ken Lang, and Mary Murrell all helped enormously in bringing this book to publication. Thanks also to Shelly Perron for her expert copyediting and to Melanie Okadigwe for her assistance in the editorial process.

There are several friends and relatives I want to thank. First of all, Carol Hill, whose talent as a writer is an inspiration and who can always make me laugh. She always came to my rescue.

Naomi Bushman, B. K. Moran, Charlie Haas, Nancy Adler, Donna Hagler, Melanie Mayer, and Arthur and Shirley Schrager all gave me help and support.

I want to express my appreciation for Roger Ebert's illuminating film reviews. Over the years, they have served as my most trustworthy guide to the movies.

I thank the University of California at Santa Cruz for giving me the freedom to pursue my intellectual interests. Barbara Laurence, Christina Cicoletti, Lin Weyers, Pam Roby, Melissa Hemler, and Ellen Borger of UCSC all helped in various ways. Cynthia Siemsen and Gretchen Wacker helped with the research.

Finally, I am deeply grateful to all the people who must remain nameless but who generously told me their love stories and whose voices you hear in this book.